Mathematical Magick:
OR, THE
WONDERS
That may be Performed by
Mechanical Geometry.

In Two Books.

CONCERNING

Mechanical { Powers. Motions.

Being one of the most Easie, Pleasant, Useful, (and yet most neglected) part of MATHEMATICKS.

Not before treated of in this Language.

By *J. Wilkins,* late L^d B^p of *Chester.*

Τέχνη κρατοῦμεν ὧν φύσει νικώμεθα.

The Fourth Edition.

LONDON:
Printed for **Ric. Baldwin,** near the
Oxford-Arms Inn, Warwick-Lane 1691.

**Kessinger Publishing's Rare Reprints
Thousands of Scarce and Hard-to-Find Books!**

We kindly invite you to view our extensive catalog list at:
http://www.kessinger.net

Printing Statement:

Due to the very old age and scarcity of this book, many of the pages may be hard to read due to the blurring of the original text, possible missing pages, missing text and other issues beyond our control.

Because this is such an important and rare work, we believe it is best to reproduce this book regardless of its original condition.

Thank you for your understanding.

Effigies Reverendi admodum veri Johannis Wilkins nuper Episcopi Cestriensis.

To His Highness the Prince Elector *Palatine*.

May it please Your Highness!

I Should not thus have presented my Diversions, where I owe my study and business; but that where all is due, a man may not justly withhold any part.

This following Discourse was composed some years since at my spare hours in the University, The Subject of it is mixed *Mathematicks; which I did the rather at such times make choice of, as being for the* pleasure *of it, more proper for recreation; and for the* facility, *more suitable to my abilities and leisure.*

I should not, Sir, have been ambitious of any so Great *(I could not of any* Better*) Patronage, had not my relation both engaged and emboldened me to this Dedication.*

They that know your Highness, how great an encourager you are, and how able

A 3   a *Judge*

The Epistle.

a Judge in all kind of ingenious Arts and Literature, must needs acknowledg your pressures and low condition to be none of the least mischiefs (amongst those many other) under which the Commonwealth of Learning does now suffer.

It would in many respects much conduce to the general advancement of religion and learning, if the reformed Churches, in whose cause and defence your family hath so deeply suffered, were but effectually mindful of their engagements to it. And particularly, if these present unhappy differences of this Nation did not occasion too much forgetfulness of their former zeal and professions for the vindicating of your family, and the restoring of your Highness; the hastning and accomplishment of which, together with the increase of all heavenly blessings upon your Highness, shall be the hearty daily prayer of

Your Highness

Most humble and most devoted
Servant and Chaplain,

JOHN WILKINS.

TO

TO THE
READER.

IT is related of *Heraclitus*, that when his Scholars had found him in a Tradesman's shop, whither they were ashamed to enter, He told them, *Quod neque tali loco dii desunt immortales*, that the gods were as well conversant in such places as in others; intimating that a divine power and wisdome might be discerned even in those common Arts, which are so much despised. And though the manual exercise and practise of them be esteemed ignoble, yet the study of their general causes and principles cannot be prejudicial to any other (tho the most sacred) profession.

It hath been my usual custom, in the course of my other studies, to propose divers Mathematical or Philosophical

To the Reader.

phical inquiries, for the recreation of my leisure-hours; and as I could gather satisfaction, to compose them to some form and method.

Some of these have been formerly published, and I have now ventured forth this discourse; wherein besides the great *delight and pleasure* (which every rational Reader must needs find in such notions as carry with them their own evidence and demonstration) there is also much *real benefit* to be learned; particularly for such Gentlemen as employ their estates in those chargeable adventures of Drawing, Mines, Cole-pits, &c. who may from hence learn the chief grounds and nature of Engines, and thereby more easily avoid the delusions of any cheating Impostor: And also for such *common Artificers*, as are well skilled in the practise of these Arts, who may be much advantaged by the right understanding of their grounds and *Theory*.

Scho. Mathem l. 2

Ramus hath observed, that the reason why *Germany* hath been so eminent

To the Reader.

nent for Mechanical inventions, is because there have been publick Lectures of this kind instituted amongst them, and those not only in the learned languages, but also in the vulgar tongue, for the capacity of every unletter'd ingenious Artificer.

This whole Discourse I call **Mathematical Magick**, because the art of such Mechanical inventions as are here chiefly insisted upon, hath been formerly so styled; and in allusion to vulgar opinion, which doth commonly attribute all such strange operations unto the power of Magick; For which reason the Ancients did name this Art Θαυματοποιητικὴ, or *Mirandorum Effectrix*.

Agrippa, De Vanit. Scient. c. 42.

The first book is called *Archimedes*, because he was the chiefest in discovering of Mechanical *powers*.

The second is styled by the name of *Dædalus*, who is related to be one of the first and most famous amongst the Ancients for his skill in making *Automata*, or self-moving Engines: both these being two of the first Authors that

To the Reader.

that did reduce Mathematical principles unto Mechanical experiments.

Other discourses of this kind, are for the most part large and voluminous, of great price and hardly gotten; and besides, there are not any of them (that I know of) in our vulgar tongue, for which these Mechanical Arts of all other are most proper. These inconveniencies are here in some measure remedied, together with the addition (if I mistake not) of divers things very considerable, and not insisted upon by others.

THE

The Contents and Method of this following Discourse.

The First Book.

Chap. 1. THE excellency of these Arts. Why they were concealed by the Ancients. The Authors that have treated of them.

Ch. 2. Concerning the name of this Art. That it may properly be styled Liberal. The subject and nature of it.

Ch. 3. Of the first Mechanical faculty, the Ballance.

Ch. 4. Concerning the second Mechanick faculty, the Leaver.

Ch. 5. How the natural motion of living creatures is conformable to these artificial rules.

Ch. 6. Concerning the Wheel.

Ch. 7.

The Contents.

Ch. 7, *Concerning the* Pulley.

Ch. 8. *Of the* Wedg.

Ch. 9. *Of the* Screw.

Ch. 10. *An inquiry into the magnificent works of the Ancients, which much exceeding our later times, may seem to infer a decay in these Mechanical arts.*

Ch. 11. *That the Ancients had divers motives and means for such vast magnificent works, which we have not.*

Ch. 12. *Concerning the force of the Mechanick faculties; particularly, the* Ballance *and* Leaver. *How they may be contrived to move the whole world, or any other conceivable weight.*

Ch. 13. *Of the* Wheel, *by multiplication of which, it is easie to move any imaginable weight.*

Ch. 14. *Concerning the infinite strength of* Wheels, Pulleys, *and* Screws;
that

The Contents.

that it is possible by the multiplication of these, to pull up an Oak by the roots with a hair, lift it up with a straw, or blow it up with ones breath, or to perform the greatest labour with the least power.

Ch. 15. *Concerning the proportion of slowness and swiftness in Mechanical motions.*

Ch. 16. *That it is possible to contrive such an artificial motion as shall be of a slowness proportionable to the swiftness of the heavens.*

Ch. 17. *Of swiftness, how it may be increased to any kind of proportion. Concerning the great force of* Archimedes *his Engines. Of the* Ballista.

Ch. 18. *Concerning the* Catapultæ, *or Engines for Arrows.*

Ch. 19. *A comparison betwixt these ancient Engines, and the Gun-powder instruments now in use.*

Ch. 20.

The Contents.

Ch. 20. *That it is possible to contrive such an artificial motion, as may be equally swift with the supposed motion of the heavens.*

The Second Book.

Ch. 1. *THE divers kinds of Automata, or Self-movers: Of Mills. Of the contrivance of several motions by rarified air. A brief digression concerning Wind-guns.*

Ch. 2. *Of a sailing Chariot, that may without horses be driven on the land by the wind, as ships are on the sea.*

Ch. 3. *Concerning the fixed Automata, Clocks, Spheres representing the heavenly motions. The several excellencies that are most commendable in such kind of contrivances.*

Ch. 4. *Of the movable and gradient Automata, representing the motion of living creatures, various sounds, of birds, or beasts, and some of them articulate.*

Ch. 5.

The Contents.

Ch. 5. *Concerning the possibility of framing an Ark for submarine Navigations. The Difficulties and Conveniences of such a contrivance.*

Ch. 6. *Of the volant Automata; Archytas his Dove, and Regiomontanus his Eagle. The possibility and great usefulness of such inventions.*

Ch. 7. *Concerning the Art of flying. The several ways whereby this hath been, or may be attempted.*

Ch. 8. *A resolution of the two chief difficulties that seem to oppose the possibility of a flying Chariot.*

Ch. 9. *Of a perpetual motion. The seeming facility and real difficulty of any such contrivance. The several ways whereby it hath been attempted, particularly by Chymistry.*

Ch. 10. *Of subterraneous Lamps, divers historical relations concerning their duration for many hundred years together.* **Ch. 11.**

The Contents.

Ch. 11 *Several opinions concerning the nature and reason of these perpetual Lamps.*

Chap. 12. *The most probable conjecture how these Lamps were framed.*

Ch. 13. *Concerning several attempts of contriving a perpetual motion by magnetical virtues.*

Chap. 14. *The seeming probability of effecting a continual motion by solid weights in a hollow wheel or sphere.*

Ch. 15. *Of composing a perpetual motion by fluid weights.* Concerning Archimedes *his water-screw. The great probability of accomplishing this inquiry by the help of that, with the fallibleness of it upon experiment.*

ARCHI-

ARCHIMEDES:
OR,
Mechanical Powers.

The First Book.

CAP. I.
The Excellency of these Arts. Why they were concealed by the Ancients. The Authors that have treated of them.

ALL those various Studies about which the sons of men do busie their endeavours, may be generally comprised under these three kinds:
$\begin{cases} \text{Divine.} \\ \text{Natural.} \\ \text{Artificial.} \end{cases}$

To

To the first of these, is reducible, not only the *speculation* of Theological Truths, but also the *practice* of those Virtues which may advantage our minds in the enquiry after their proper happiness. And these Arts alone may truly be stiled Liberal, *Quæ liberum faciunt hominem, quibus curæ virtus est*, (saith the Divine Stoick) which set a man at liberty from his lusts and passions.

Sen Ep. 88.

To the Second, may be referred all that knowledge which concerns the frame of this great Universe, or the usual course of Providence in the government of these created things.

To the Last, do belong all those Inventions, whereby Nature is any way quickned or advanced in her defects: These Artificial Experiments being (as it were) but so many Essays, whereby men do naturally attempt to restore themselves from the first general curse inflicted upon their Labours.

This following Discourse does properly appertain to this latter kind. Now

Cap. 1. *Mechanical Powers.*

Now Art may be said either to *imitate* Nature, as in Limning and Pictures; or to *help* Nature, as in Medicine; or to *overcome* and *advance* Nature, as in these Mechanical Disciplines, which in this respect are by so much to be preferred before the other, by how much their end and power is more excellent. Nor are they therefore to be esteemed less noble, because more practical, since our best and most divine knowledge is intended for action; and those may justly be counted barren studies, which do not conduce to Practice as their proper end.

But so apt are we to contemn every thing which is common, that the ancient Philosophers esteemed it a great part of Wisdom, to conceal their Learning from vulgar apprehension or use, thereby the better to maintain it in its due honour and respect. And therefore did they generally vail all their Arts and Sciences under such mystical expressions, as might excite the peoples wonder

B 2 and

and reverence, fearing left a more easie and familiar discovery, might expose them to contempt. *Sic ipsa mysteria fabularum cuniculis operiuntur, summatibus tantum viris, sapientia interprete, veri arcani conscius; Contenti sint reliqui, ad venerationem, figuris defendentibus à vilitate secretum,* saith a Platonick.

<small>Macrobius Somn. Scip. l. 1. c. 2.</small>

Hence was it, that the ancient Mathematicians did place all their learning in abstracted speculations, refusing to debase the principles of that noble Profession unto Mechanical Experiments. Insomuch, that those very Authors amongst them, who were most eminent for their inventions of this kind, and were willing by their own practice, to manifest unto the world those Artificial wonders that might be wrought by these Arts, as *Dædalus, Archytas, Archimedes,* &c. were notwithstanding so much infected with this blind superstition, as not to leave any thing in writing concerning the grounds and manner of these operations.

Quin-

Cap. 1. *Mechanical Powers.*

Quintilian speaking to this purpose of *Archimedes*, saith thus: *Quamvis tantum tamque singularem Geometriæ usum, Archimedes, singularibus exemplis, & admirandis operibus ostenderit, propter quæ non humanæ sed divinæ Scientiæ laudem sit adeptus, hæsit tamen in illa Platonis persuasione, nec ullam Mechanicam literam prodere voluit.*

By which means, Posterity hath unhappily lost, not only the benefit of those particular discoveries, but also the proficiency of those Arts in general. For when once the learned men did forbid the reducing of them to particular use and vulgar experiment, others did thereupon refuse these studies themselves, as being but empty and useless speculations. Whence it came to pass, that the Science of Geometry was so universally neglected, receiving little or no addition for many hundred years together.

Amongst these Ancients, the divine *Plato* is observed to be one of the greatest sticklers for this fond opinion,

Quint. I. 1. c. 10.

Per. Ram. Schol. Mathem. l. 1.

opinion, severely dehorting all his followers from prostituting Mathematical Principles, unto common apprehension or practice. Like the envious Emperour *Tiberius*, who is reported to have killed an Artificer for making glass malleable, fearing lest thereby the price of Metals might be debased. So he, in his superstition to Philosophy, would rather chuse to deprive the world of all those useful and excellent Inventions which might be thence contrived, than to expose that Profession unto the contempt of the ignorant vulgar.

Plin. Nat. l.36. c.26.

But his Scholar *Aristotle*, (as in many other particulars, so likewise in this) did justly oppose him, and became himself one of the first Authors that hath writ any methodical Discourse concerning these Arts; chusing rather a certain and general benefit, before the hazard that might accrue from the vain and groundless disrespects of some ignorant persons. Being so far from esteeming Geometry dishonoured by the application

Arist. Quæst. Mechan.

Cap. 1. *Mechanical Powers.*

on of it to Mechanical practises, that he rather thought it to be thereby adorned as with curious variety, and to be exalted unto its natural end. And whereas the Mathematicians of those former ages, did possess all their Learning, as covetous men do their Wealth, only in thought and notion; the judicious *Aristotle*, like a wise Steward, did lay it out to particular use and improvement, rightly preferring the reality and substance of publick benefit, before the shadows of some retired speculation, or vulgar opinion.

Since him, there have been divers other Authors, who have been eminent for their Writings of this nature. Such were *Hero Alexandrinus, Hero Mechanicus, Pappus Alexandrinus, Proclus Mathematicus, Vitruvius, Guidus Ubaldus, Henricus Monantholius, Galilæus, Guevara, Mersennus, Bettinus*, &c. Besides many others, that have treated largely of several Engines, as *Augustine Ramelli, Vittorio Zoncha, Jacobus Bessonius, Vegetius, Lipsius.*

Most

Most of which Authors I have perused, and shall willingly acknowledge my self a debtor to them for many things in this following Discourse.

CAP. II.

Concerning the Name of this Art. That it may properly be styled Liberal. The subject and nature of it.

The word *Mechanick* is thought to be derived ἀπὸ τῶ μῆκες ἀνύειν, *multum ascendere, pertingere:* intimating the efficacy and force of such Inventions. Or else παρὰ μὴ χαίνειν (saith *Eustathius*) *quia hiscere non sinit,* because these Arts are so full of pleasant variety, that they admit not either of sloth or weariness.

According to ordinary signification, the word is used in opposition to the Liberal Arts; whereas in propriety of speech those employments alone may be styled *Illiberal*, which require only some bodily exercise, as Manufactures, Trades, &c. And on the con-

Lypsius Pplyorcet. l. 1. Dialog. 3. That's a senseless absurd Etymology imposed by some, Quia intellectus in eis mœchatur, as if these arts did prostitute and adulterate the Understanding.

contrary, that difcipline which difcovers the general caufes, effects, and properties of things, may truly be efteemed as a *fpecies* of Philofophy.

But here it fhould be noted, that this Art is ufually diftinguifhed into a twofold kind:

1. *Rational.*
2. *Cheirurgical.*

The *Rational* is that which treats of thofe Principles and Fundamental Notions, which may concern thefe Mechanical practifes.

The *Cheirurgical*, or *Manual*, doth refer to the making of thefe Inftruments, and the exercifing of fuch particular Experiments. As in the works of Architecture, Fortifications, and the like.

The firft of thefe, is the fubject of this Difcourfe, and may properly be ftiled *Liberal*, as juftly deferving the profecution of an ingenuous mind. For if we confider it according to its birth and original, we fhall find it to fpring from honourable Parentage, being produced by *Geometry* on the one

Pappus Proem. in Collect. Mathem. *l.* 8.

one side, and *Natural Philosophy* on the other. If according to its use and benefit, we may then discern, that to this should be referred all those Arts and Professions so necessary for humane society, whereby Nature is not only directed in her usual course, but sometimes also commanded against her own law. The particulars that concern Architecture, Navigation, Husbandry, Military affairs, &c. are most of them reducible to this Art, both for their invention and use.

Those other disciplines of Logick, Rhetorick, &c. do not more protect and adorn the mind, than these Mechanical powers do the body.

And therefore are they well worthy to be entertained with greater industry and respect, than they commonly meet with in these times; wherein there be very many that pretend to be Masters in all the Liberal Arts, who scarce understand any thing in these particulars.

The subject of this Art is concerning the heaviness of several bodies,

Cap. 2. *Mechanical Powers.*

or the proportion that is required betwixt any weight, in relation to the power which may be able to move it. And so it refers likewise to violent and artificial motion, as Philosophy doth to that which is natural.

The proper end for which this Art is intended, is to teach how by understanding the true difference betwixt the *Weight* and the *Power*, a man may add such a fitting supplement to the strength of the Power, that it shall be able to move any conceivable Weight, though it should never so much exceed that force which the Power is naturally endowed with.

The Art it self may be thus described to be a Mathematical Discipline, which by the help of Geometrical Principles, do teach to contrive several Weights and Powers, unto any kind either of motion or rest, according as the Artificer shall determine.

If it be doubted how this may be esteemed a *species* of Mathematicks, whenas it treats of Weights, and not of

Dav. Rivaltus præf. in lib. Archimed. de centro gravitatis.

of *Quantity*; For satisfaction to this, there are two particulars considerable.

1. *Mathematicks* in its latitude is usually divided into *pure* and *mixed*: And though the *pure* do handle only *abstract quantity* in the *general*, as *Geometry*, *Arithmetick*; yet that which is *mixed*, doth consider the quantity of some *particular determinate* subject. So *Astronomy* handles the quantity of Heavenly motions, *Musick* of sounds, and *Mechanicks* of weights and powers.

2. Heaviness or Weight is not here considered, as being such a natural *quality*, whereby condensed bodies do of themselves *tend downwards*; but rather as being an affection, whereby they may be measured. And in this sense *Aristotle* himself refers it amongst the other *species* of *quantity*, as having the same proper essence, which is to be compounded of integral parts. So a pound doth consist of ounces, drams, scruples. Whence it is evident, that there is not any such repugnancy in the subject of this Art, as may hinder it from being a true *species* of *Mathematicks*.

Metaph. l. 10. c. 2.

CAP.

CAP. III.

Of the first Mechanical Faculty, the Ballance.

THE Mechanical Faculties, by which the Experiments of this nature must be contrived, are usually reckoned to be these six:

1. *Libra.*	1. *The Ballance.*
2. *Vectis.*	2. *The Leaver.*
3. *Axis in Peritrochio.*	3. *The Wheel.*
4. *Trochlea.*	4. *The Pulley.*
5. *Cuneus.*	5. *The Wedg.*
6. *Cochlea.*	6. *The Screw.*

Unto some of which, the force of all Mechanical Inventions must necessarily be reduced. I shall speak of them severally, and in this order.

First concerning the Ballance; this and the Leaver are usually confounded together, as being but one faculty, because the general grounds and proportions of either force is so exactly the same. But for better distinction, and more

more clear discovery of their natures, I shall treat of them severally.

The first invention of the Ballance is commonly attributed to *Astrea*, who is therefore deified for the goddess of Justice; and that Instrument it self advanced amongst the Cœlestial signs.

The particulars concerning it, are so commonly known, and of such easie experiment, that they will not need any large explication. The chief end and purpose of it, is for the distinction of several ponderosities; For the understanding of which, we must note, that if the length of the sides in the Ballance, and the weights at the ends of them, be both mutually equal, then the Beam will be in a horizontal scituation. But on the contrary, if either the weights alone be equal, and not their distances, or the distances alone, and not the weights, then the Beam will accordingly decline.

As in this following diagram.

Sup-

Cap. 3. *Mechanical Powers.* 15

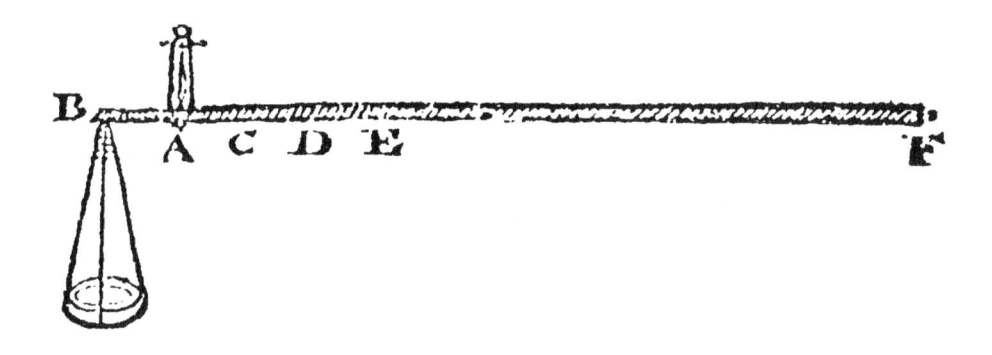

Suppose an equal weight at *C*, unto that at *B*, (which points are both equally distant from the center *A*,) it is evident that then the beam *B F*, will hang horizontally. But if the weight supposed at *C*, be unequal to that at *B*, or if there be an equal weight at *D E*, or any of the other unequal distances; the Beam must then necessarily decline.

With this kind of Ballance, it is usual by the help only of one weight, to measure sundry different gravities, whether more or less than that by which they are measured. As by the example here described, a man may with one pound alone, weigh any other body within ten pounds, because the heaviness of any weight

Cardan, Subtil. l.1.

doth

doth increase proportionably to its distance from the Center. Thus one pound at *D*, will equiponderate unto two pounds at *B*, because the distance *AD*, is double unto *AB*. And for the same reason, one pound at *E*, will equiponderate to three pounds at *B*; and one pound at *F*, unto ten at *B*, because there is still the same disproportion betwixt their several distances

This kind of Ballance is usually styled *Romana, statere*. It seems to be of ancient use, and is mentioned by *Aristotle* under the name of φάλαγξ.

Hence it is easie to apprehend, how that false Ballance may be composed, so often condemned by the Wiseman, as being an abomination to the Lord. If the sides of the Beam be not equally divided, as suppose one have 10 parts, and the other 11, then any two weights that differ according to this proportion, (the heavier being placed on the shorter side, and the lighter on the longer) will equiponderate. And yet both the scales being empty, shall hang in *æquilibrio*,

as

Mechan. c. 21.

Prov. 11. 1. c. 16. 11. Item cap. 20. 10, 23. Pappus Collect. Mathem. l. 8.

Cap. 3. Mechanical Powers. 17

as if they were exactly juſt and true, as in this deſcription.

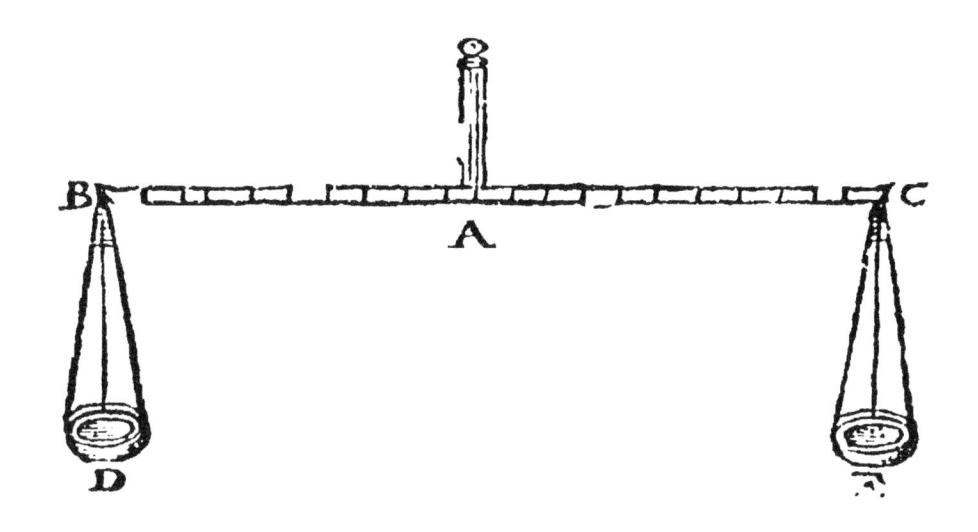

Suppoſe *AC*, to have 11 ſuch parts, whereof *AB*, has but 10, and yet both of them to be in themſelves of equal weight; it is certain, that whether the ſcales be empty, or whether in the ſcale *D*, we put 1 pound, and at *E* 10 pound, yet both of them ſhall equiponderate, becauſe there is juſt ſuch a diſproportion in the length of the ſides; *AC*, being unto *AB*, as 11 to 10.

The frequency of ſuch cozenages in theſe dayes, may be evident from common experience: and that they were uſed alſo in former ages, may

C appear

appear from *Aristotle's* testimony concerning the Merchants in his time. For the remedying of such abuses the Ancients did appoint divers Officers styled ζυγοσάται, who were to overlook the common measures.

So great care was there amongst the Jews for the preservation of commutitive justice from all abuse and falsification in this kind, that the publick standards and originals by which all other measures were to be tryed and allowed, were with much religion preserved in the Sanctuary, the care of them being committed to the Priests and Levites, whose office it was to look unto *all manner of measures and size*. Hence is that frequent expression, *According to the shekel of the Sanctuary*; and that Law, *All thy estimations shall be according to the shekel of the Sanctuary*; which doth not refer to any weight or coin, distinct from, and more than the vulgar, (as some fondly conceive) but doth only oblige men in their dealing and traffique to make use of such just

Marginalia: Quæstion. Mechan. c 2. Budæus. *Hence the proverb,* Zygostatica fides. 1 Chron. 23. 29. Exod. 30. 3 Lev. 27 25

Cap. 3. Mechanical Powers.

just measures, as were agreeable unto the publick standards that were kept in the Sanctuary.

The manner how such deceitful ballances may be discovered, is by changing the weights into each other scale, and then the inequality will be manifest.

From the former grounds rightly apprehended, it is easie to conceive how a man may find out the just proportion of a weight, which in any point given, shall equiponderate to several weights given, hanging in several places of the Beam.

Some of these Ballances are made so exact, (those especially which the Refiners use) as to be sensibly turned with the eightieth part of a grain: which (though it may seem very strange) is nothing to what * *Capellus* relates of one at *Sedan*, that would turn with the four hundredth part of a grain.

There are several contrivances to make use of these in measuring the weight of blows, the force of powder,

Master Greaves Roman foot.
* *De ponderibus & nummis, l. 1.*

the strength of strings, or other oblong substances, condensed air, the distinct proportion of several metals mixed together, the different gravity of divers bodies in the water, from what they have in the open air, with divers the like ingenious inquiries.

CAP. IV.

Concerning the Second Mechanick faculty, the Leaver.

<small>Aristotle Quæst. Mechan. cap. 4. Archimedes, de Æquipond. rant. l. 1. prop. 7. Vitruvius Architect. l. 10. c. 8.</small>

THE second Mechanical faculty, is the Leaver; the first invention of it is usually ascribed to *Neptune*, and represented by his Trident, which in the Greek are both called by one name, and are not very unlike in form, being both of them somewhat broader at one end, than in the other parts.

There is one main principle concerning it, which is (as it were) the very sum and epitome of this whole art. The meaning of it is thus expressed by *Aristotle*, ὃ τὸ κινούμενον βάρος πρὸς τὸ κινοῦν τὸ μῆκος πρὸς ἀντιπέπονθεν. That is,

Cap. 4. *Mechanical Powers.*

is, as the weight is to an equivalent power, so is the distance betwixt the weight and the center, unto the distance betwixt the center and the power, and so reciprocally. Or thus, the power that doth equiponderate with any weight, must have the same proportion unto it, as there is betwixt their several distances from the center or fulciment: as in this folowing figure.

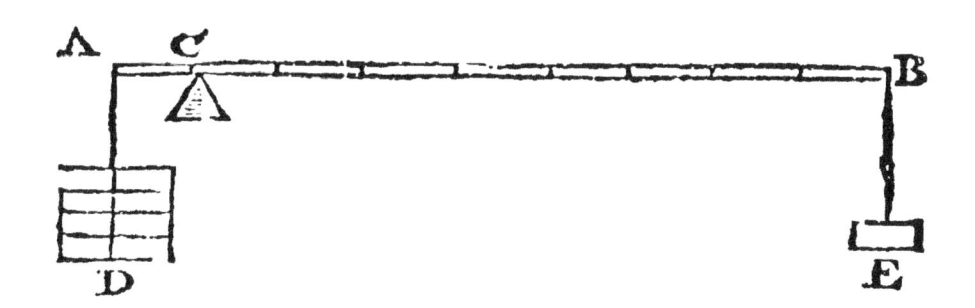

Where suppose the Leaver to be represented by the length *A B*, the center or * prop at the point *C*, the weight to be sustained *D*, the power that doth uphold it *E*.

Now the meaning of the foresaid principle doth import thus much, that the power at *E*, must bear the same

* *This Aristotle calls* ὑπομόχλιον. *Vitruvius* pressio. *Ubaldus* Fulcimentum, *Dan. Barbarus,* Scabellum

same proportion to the Weight *D*, as the distance *C A*, doth to the other *C B*; which, because it is octuple in the present example, therefore it will follow that one pound at *B*, or *E*, will equiponderate to eight pounds at *A*, or *D*, as is expressed in the figure. The ground of which maxime is this, because the point *C*, is supposed to be the center of gravity, on either side of which, the parts are of equal weight.

And this kind of proportion is not only to be observed when the power doth *press downwards*, (as in the former example) but also in the other species of violent motion, as *lifting, drawing,* and the like. Thus if the prop or fulciment were supposed to be at the extremity of the Leaver,

Cap. 4. *Mechanical Powers.*

as in this Diagram at *A*, then the weight *B*, would require such a difference in the strengths or powers that did sustain it, as there is betwixt the several distances *A C*, and *B C*. For as the distance *A B*, is unto *A C*, so is the power at *C*, to the weight at *B*; that is, the power at *A*, must be double to that at *C*, because the distance *B C*, is twice as much as *B A*. from whence it is easie to conceive, how any burden carried betwixt two persons, may be proportioned according to their different strengths. If the weight were imagined to hang at the number 2, then the power at *C*, would sustain but two of those parts, whereof that at *A*, did uphold 16. If it be supposed at the figure (3) then the strength at *C*, to that at *A*, would be but as three to fifteen. But if it were situated at the figure (9) then each of the extremities would participate of it alike, because that being the middle, both the distances are equal. If at the number (12) then the strength at *C*, is required to be

The right understanding of this doth much conduce to the explication of the Pulley.

double

double unto that at *A.* and in the like manner are we to conceive of the other intermediate divisions.

Thus also must it be, if we suppose the power to be placed betwixt the fulciment and the weight, as in this example.

Where, as *AC*, is to *AB*, so is the power at *B*, to the weight at *C*.

Hence likewise may we conceive the reason why it is so much harder to carry any long substance, either on the shoulders, or in the hand, if it be held by either of the extremes, than if it be sustained by the middle of it. The strength that must equiponderate at the nearer end, sometimes increasing the weight almost double to what it is in it self.

Imagine

Cap. 4. *Mechanical Powers.*

Imagine the point *A*, to be the place where any long substance (as suppose a Pike) is sustained, it is evident from the former principle, that the strength at *B*, (which makes it lye level) must be equal to all the length *A C*, which is almost the whole Pike.

And as it is in the depressing, or elevating, so likewise is it in the drawing of any weight, as a Coach, Plow, or the like.

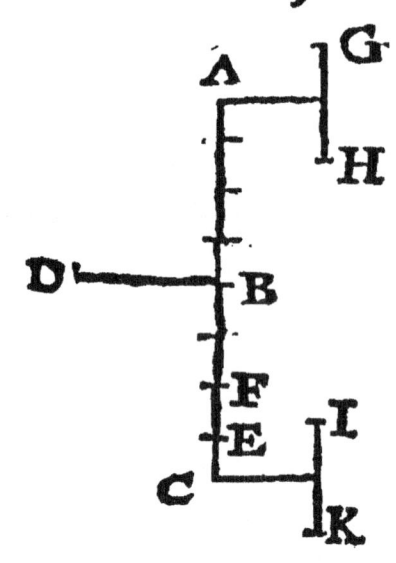

Let the line *D B*, represent the Pole or Carriage on which the burden is sustained, and the line *A C*, the cross barr; at each of its extremities, there is a several spring tree *G H*, and *I K*, to which either horses or oxen may be fastned. Now because *A*, and *C*, are equally distant from the middle *B*, therefore in this case the strength must be equal on both sides; but if we suppose one of these spring-trees to be fastned unto the points *E*, or *F*, then the strength required to draw on that side, will be so much more, as the distance *E B*, or *F B*, is less than that of *A B*; that is, either as three or four, as *E B*, to *B A*,

Cap. 4. *Mechanical Powers.*

B A, or as one to two, as *F B*, to *B A*. So that the beast fastned at *A*, will not draw so much by a quarter, as the other at *E*, and but half as much as one at *F*.

Whence it is easie to conceive how a husbandman (*cum inæquales veniunt ad aratra juvenci*) may proportion the labour of drawing according to the several strength of his Oxen.

Unto this Mechanical faculty should be reduced sundry other instruments in common use. Thus the Oars, Stearn, Masts, &c. according to their force, whereby they give motion to the ship, are to be conceived under this head.

Thus likewise for that engine, whereby Brewers and Dyers do commonly draw water, which *Aristotle* calls ηλόνειον, and others *Tellenon*. This being the same kind of Instrument, by which *Archimedes* drew up the ships of *Marcellus*.

Arist. Mechan. c 5, 6, 7. Vide Guevar. Comment.

Mechan. c. 29. Pet. Grinitus, de honesta Disciplina l. 19. c. 2. *calls it corruptly* Tellenon.

C A P.

CAP. V.

How the natural motion of living creatures is conformable to these artificial rules.

THE former Principle being already explained, concerning artificial and dead motions, it will not be altogether impertinent, if in the next place we apply it unto those that are natural in living bodies, and examine whether these also are not governed by the same kind of proportions.

In all perfect living creatures, there is a twofold kind of motive instruments.

1. Primary, the Muscles.
2. Secondary, the Members.

The Muscles are naturally fitted to be instruments of motion, by the manner of their frame and composure; consisting of flesh as their chief material, and besides of Nerves, Ligatures, Veins, Arteries, and Membrances.

The

Cap. 5. Mechanical Powers.

The *Nerves* serve for the conveyance of the motive faculty from the brain. The *Ligatures* for the strengthning of them, that they may not flag and languish in their motions. The *Veins* for their nourishment. The *Arteries* for the supplying of them with spirit, and natural vigor. The *Membrances* for the comprehension or inclosure of all these together, and for the distinction of one muscle from another. There are besides divers *fibræ* or hairy substances, which Nature hath bestowed for the farther corroborating of their motions; these being dispersed through every muscle, do so joyn together in the end of them, as to make intire nervous bodies, which are called *Tendones*, almost like the grisles. Now this (saith *Galen*) may fitly be compared to the broader part of the Leaver, that is put under the weight, which, as it ought to be so much the stronger, by how much it is put to a greater force; so likewise by this doth nature inable the muscles and nerves for

De Placit. Hippoc. & Platon. l. 10. c. 10.

for those motions, which otherwise would be too difficult for them.

Whence it may evidently appear, that according to the opinion of that eminent Phisician, these natural motions are regulated by the like grounds with the artificial.

2. Thus also is it in those secondary instruments of motion, the members: amongst which, the hand is ὄργανον ὀργάνων, the instrument of instruments (as *Galen* styles it); and as the soul of man doth bear in it the image of the divine wisdom and providence, so this part of the body seems in some sort to represent the Omnipotency of God, whilst it is able to perform such various and wonderful effects by the help of this art. But now for its own proper natural strength, in the lifting any great weight, this is always proportioned according to its extension from the body, being of least force when it is fully stretched out, or at arms end, (as we say) because then the shoulder joynt is as the center of

De usu-partium l. I. c. 2.

its

its motion, from which, the hand in that posture, being very remote, the weight of any thing it holds must be accordingly augmented. Whereas the arm being drawn in, the elbow-joynt doth then become its center, which will diminish the weight proportionably, as that part is nearer unto it than the other.

To this purpose also, there is another subtil probleme proposed by *Aristotle*, concerning the postures of sitting and rising up. The quære is this, Why a man cannot rise up from his seat, unless he first, either bend his body forward, or thrust his feet backward.

Mechan. c. 31

In the posture of sitting, our legs are supposed to make a right angle with our thighs, and they with our backs, as in this figure.

Where

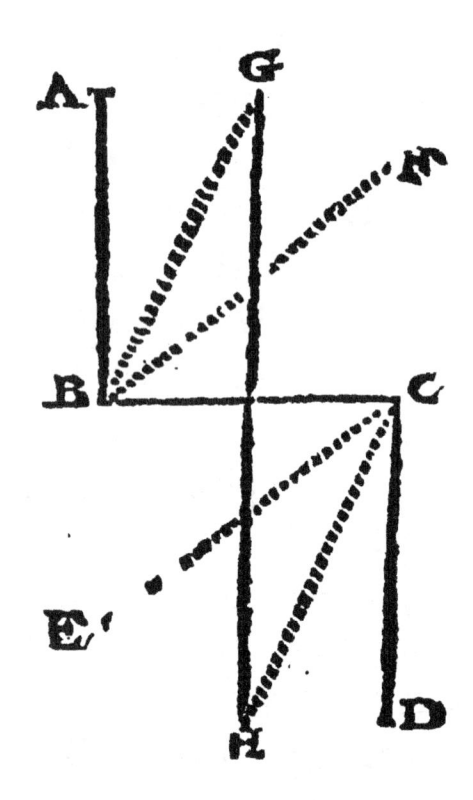

Where let *A B* represent the back, *B C* the thighs, *C D* the legs. Now it is evident, that a man cannot rise from this posture, unless either the back *A B*, do first incline unto *F*, to make an acute angle with the thighs *B C* ; or else that the legs *C D*, do incline towards *E*, which may also make an acute angle with the thighs *B C* ; or lastly, unless both of them do decline to the points *G H*, where they may be included in the same perpendicular.

For

Cap. 5. Mechanical Powers.

For the resolution of which, the Philosopher proposes these two particulars.

1. A right angle (saith he) is a kind of equality, and that being naturally the cause of rest, must needs be an impediment to the motion of rising.

2. Because when either of the parts are brought into an acute angle, the head being removed over the feet, or they under the head; in such a posture the whole man is much nearer disposed to the form of standing, wherein all these parts are in one straight perpendicular line, than he is by the other of right angles, in which the back and legs are two parallels; or that of turning these straight angles into obtuse, which would not make an erect posture, but declining.

But neither of these particulars (as I conceive) do fully satisfie the present quære, neither do the Commentators, *Monantholius*, or *Guevara*, better resolve it. Rather suppose B C, to be as a Vectis or Leaver, to-

D wards

wards the middle of which is the place of the fulciment, *A B*, as the weight, *C D*, the power that is to raise it.

Now the body being situate in this rectangular form, the weight *A B*, must needs be augmented proportionably to its distance from the fulciment, which is about half the thighs; whereas if we suppose either the weight to be inclined unto *F*, or the power to *E*, or both of them to *G H*, then there is nothing to be lifted up, but the bare weight it self, which in this situation is not at all increased with any addition by distance.

For in these conclusions concerning the Leaver, we must always imagine that point which is touched by a perpendicular from the center of gravity, to be one of the terms. So that the diverse elevation or depression of the instrument, will infer a great alteration in the weight it self, as may more clearly be discerned by this following Diagram.

Where

Cap. 5. *Mechanical Powers.*

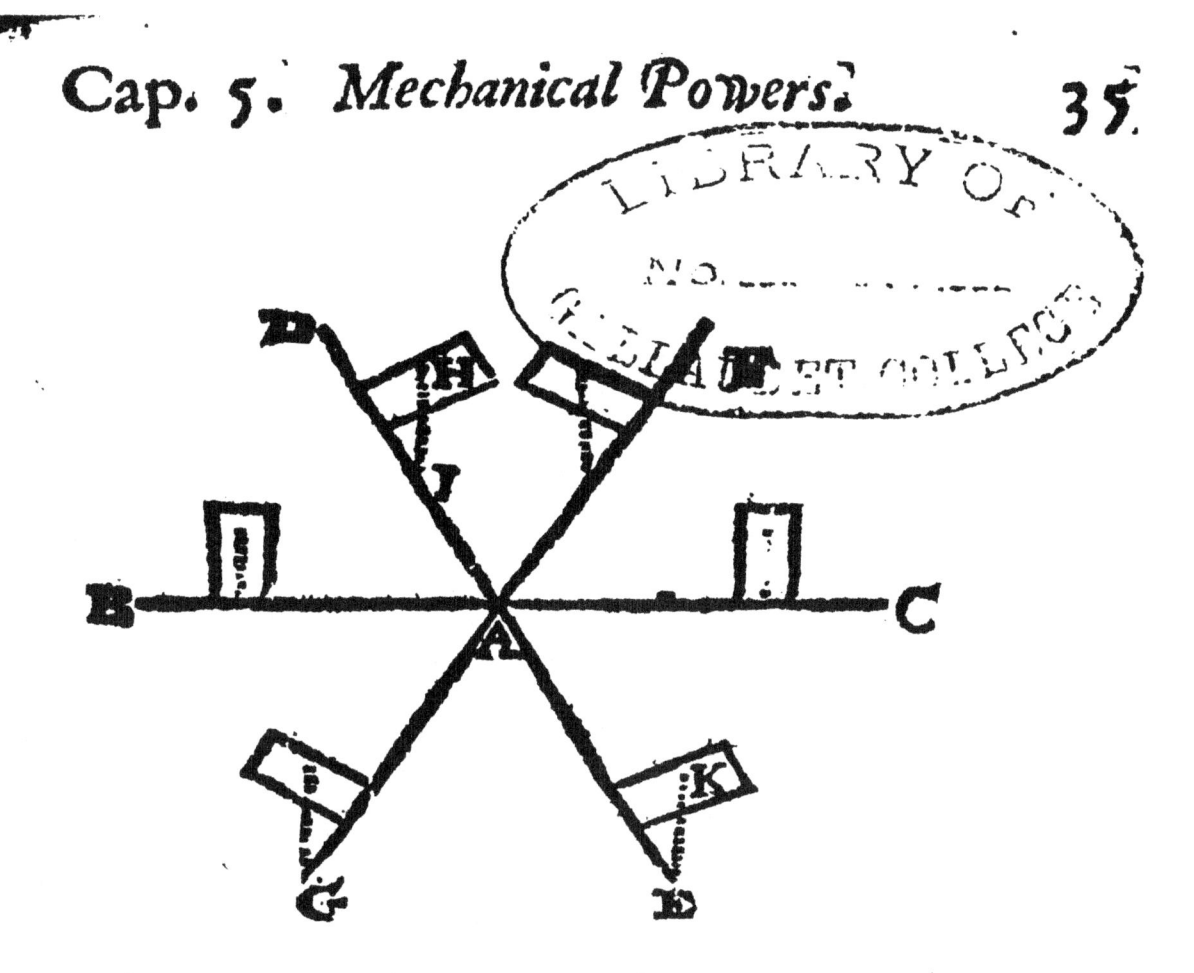

Where *A* is fuppofed to be the place of the prop or fulciment; *B C* a Leaver which ftands horizontally, the power and the weight belonging unto it, being equal both in themfelves, and alfo in their diftances from the prop.

But now fuppofe this inftrument to be altered according to the fituation *D E*, then the weight *D* will be diminifhed, by fo much, as the perpendicular from its center of gravity

vity *H I*, doth fall nearer to the prop or fulciment at *A*. And the power at *E*, will be so much augmented, as the perpendicular from its center *K E* does fall farther from the point at *A*. And so on the contrary in that other situation of the Leaver *F G*; whence it is easie to conceive the true reason why the inclining of the body, or the putting back of the leg, should so much conduce to the facility of rising.

Sir Franc. Bacon's Nat. Hist. Exp. 731.

From these grounds likewise may we understand, why the knees should be most weary in ascending, and the thighs in descending; which is because the weight of the body doth bear most upon the knee joints, in raising it self up, and most upon the muscles of the thighs, when it stays it self in coming down.

There are divers other natural problems to this purpose, which I forbear to recite. We do not so much as go, or sit, or rise, without the use of this Mechanical Geometry.

CAP.

Cap. 6. *Mechanical Powers.* 37

CAP. VI.
Concerning the Wheel.

THE third Mechanical faculty is commonly ſtiled *axis in peritrochio.* It conſiſts of an axis or Cylinder, having a rundle about it, wherein there are faſtned divers ſpokes, by which the whole may be turn'd round, according to this figure.

Called likewiſe ὄνος Ariſt. Mechan. c. 14.

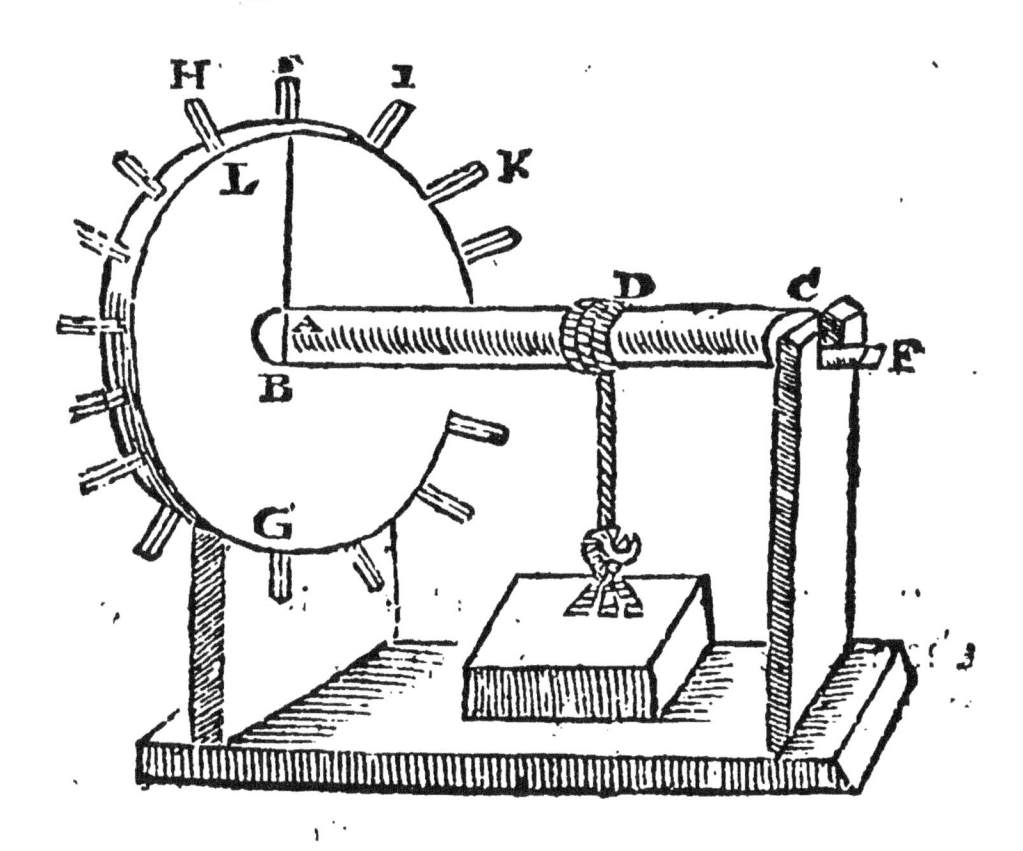

D 3 Where

Where *B C* does represent the Cylinder which is supposed to move upon a smaller Axis at *E*, (this being all one in comparison to the several proportions, as if it were a meer Mathematical line) *L G*, is the rundle or wheel, *H F I K*, several spokes or handles that are fastned in it; *D*, the place where the cord is fastned for the drawing or lifting up of any weight.

The force of this instrument doth consist in that disproportion of distance, which there is betwixt the Semidiameter of the Cylinder *A B*, and the Semidiameter of the rundle with the spokes *F A*. For let us conceive the line *F B*, to be as a Leaver, wherein *A* is the center or fulciment, *B* the place of the weight, and *F* of the power. Now it is evident from the former principles, that by how much the distance *F A*, is greater than *A B*, by so much less need the power be at *F*, in respect of the weight at *B*. Suppose *A B* to be as the tenth part of *A F*, then the power

Cap. 6. *Mechanical Powers.* 39

er or strength which is but as a hundred pound at *F*, will be equal to a thousand pound at *B*.

For the clearer explication of this faculty, it will not be amiss to consider the form of it, as it will appear, being more fully exposed to the view. As in this other Diagram.

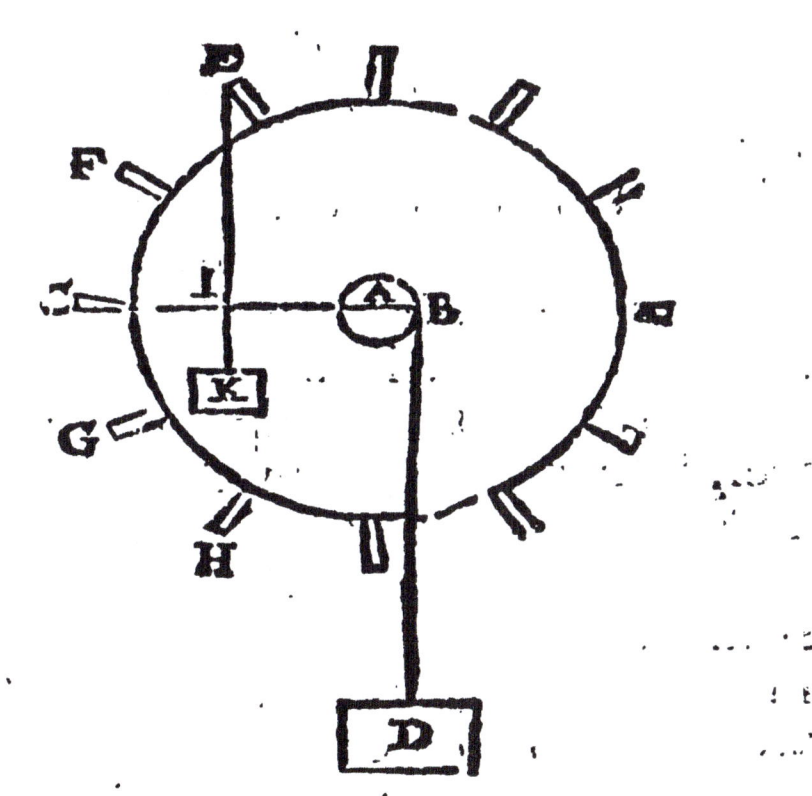

Suppose *A B* for the Semidiameter of the Axis or Cylinder, and *A C* for the Semidiameter of the rundle, with the spokes; then the power

at

at *C*, which will be able to support the weight *D*, must bear the same proportion unto it, as *A B* doth to *A C*; so that by how much shorter the distance *A B* is, in comparison to the distance *A C*, by so much less need the power be at *C*, which may be able to support the weight *D*, hanging at *B*.

And so likewise is it for the other spokes or handles *E F G H*, at either of which, if we conceive any power which shall move according to the same circumference wherein these handles are placed, then the strength of this power will be all one, as if it were at *C*. But now supposing a dead weight hanging at any of them, (as at *E*,) then the disproportion will vary. The power being so much less than that at *C*, by how much the line *A C* is longer than *A I*. The weight *K*, being of the same force at *E*, as if it were hung at *I*, in which point the perpendicular of its gravity doth cut the Diameter.

The chief advantage which this in-

Cap. 6. Mechanical Powers.

instrument doth bestow, above that of the Leaver, doth consist in this particular. In a Leaver, the motion can be continued only for so short a space, as may be answerable to that little distance betwixt the fulciment and the weight: which is always by so much lesser, as the disproportion betwixt the weight and the power is greater, and the motion it self more easie. But now in this invention, that inconvenience is remedied; for by a frequent rotation of the axis, the weight may be moved for any height or length, as occasion shall require.

Unto this faculty may we refer the force of all those engines which consist of wheels with teeth in them.

Hence also may we discern the reason why sundry instruments in common use, are framed after the like form with the following figures.

All

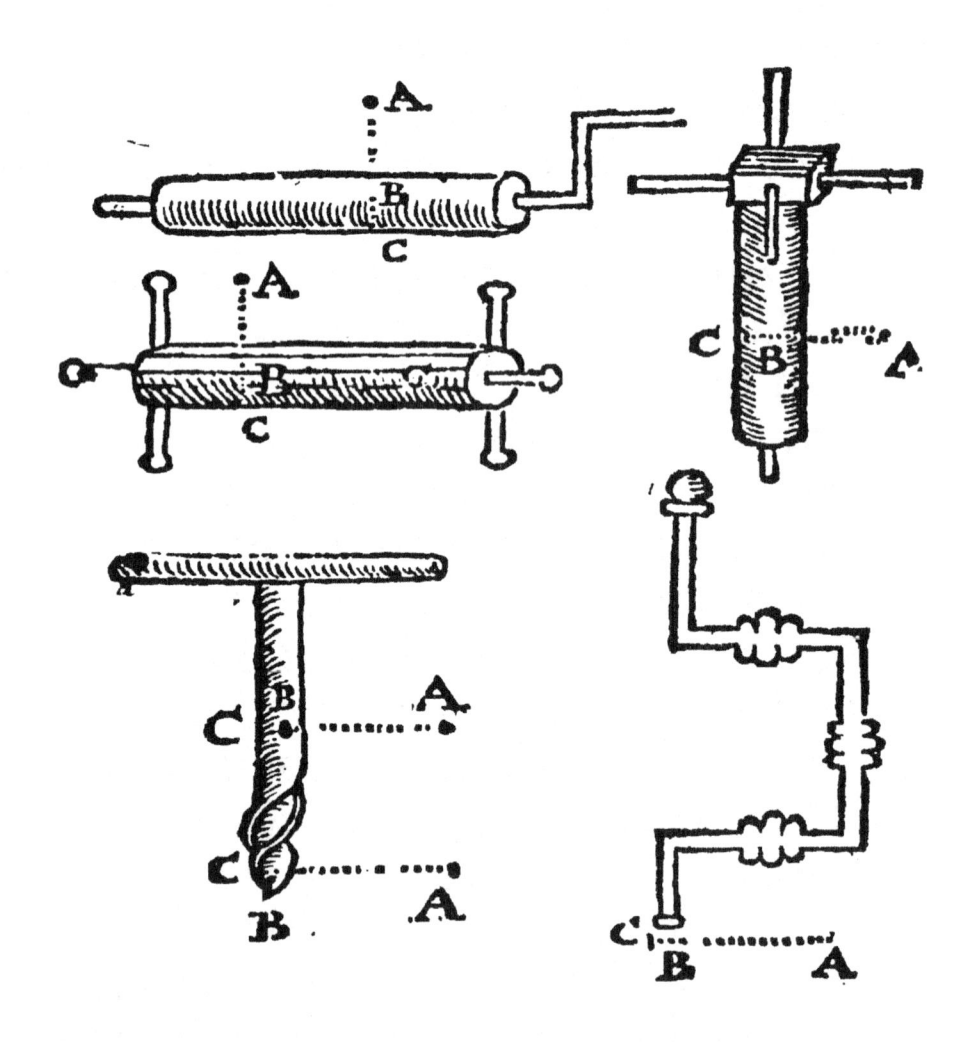

All which are but several kinds of this third Mechanical faculty. In which the points *A B C*, do represent the places of the power, the fulciment, and the weight. The power being in the same proportion unto the weight, as *B C* is unto *B A*.

CAP.

CAP. VII.

Concerning the Pulley.

THat which is reckon'd for the fourth Faculty, is the Pulley: which is of such ordinary use, that it needs not any particular description. The chief parts of it are divers little rundles, that are moveable about their proper axes. These are usually divided according to their several situations, into the upper and lower. If an engine have two of these rundles above, and two below, it is usually called δίσπαςΘ, if three τρίσπαςος, if many, πολύσπαςος.

Arist. Mechan. c. 19.

The lower Pulleys only do give force to the motion. If we suppose a weight to hang upon any of the upper rundles, it will then require a power, that in it self shall be fully equal for the sustaining of it.

The

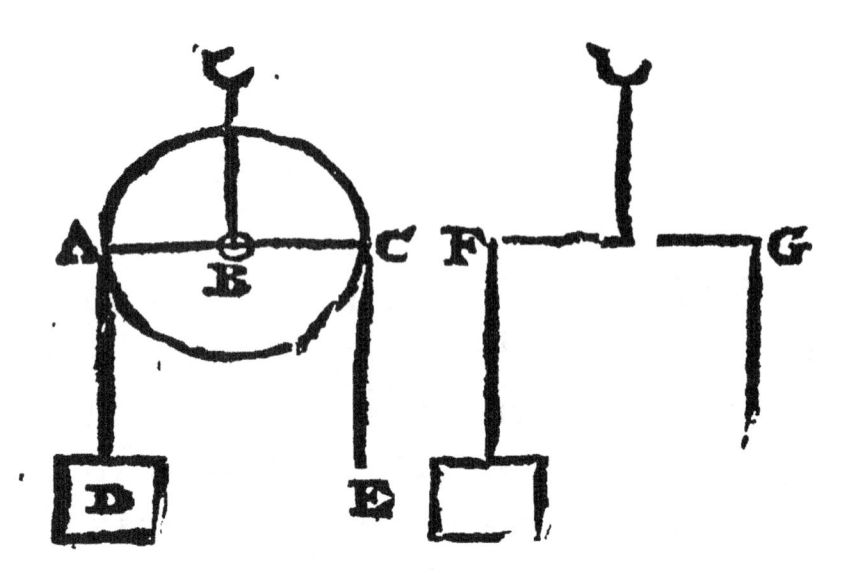

The Diamiter *AC*, being as the beam of a ballance, of which *B* is the proper center. Now the parts *A*, and *C*, being equally diftant from this center, therefore the power at *E*, muft be equal to the weight at *D*, it being all one as if the power and the weight were faftned by two feveral ftrings at the ends of the ballance *F G*.

Now all the upper Pulleys being of the fame nature, it muft necefſarily follow, that none of them do in themfelves conduce to the eafing of the power, or lightning the weight, but only for the greater conveniency

Cap. 7. *Mechanical Powers.* 45

cy of the motion, the cords by this means being more easily moved than otherwise they would.

But now suppose the weight to be sustained above the Pulley, as it is in all those of the lower sort; and then the power which supports it, need be but half as much as the weight it self.

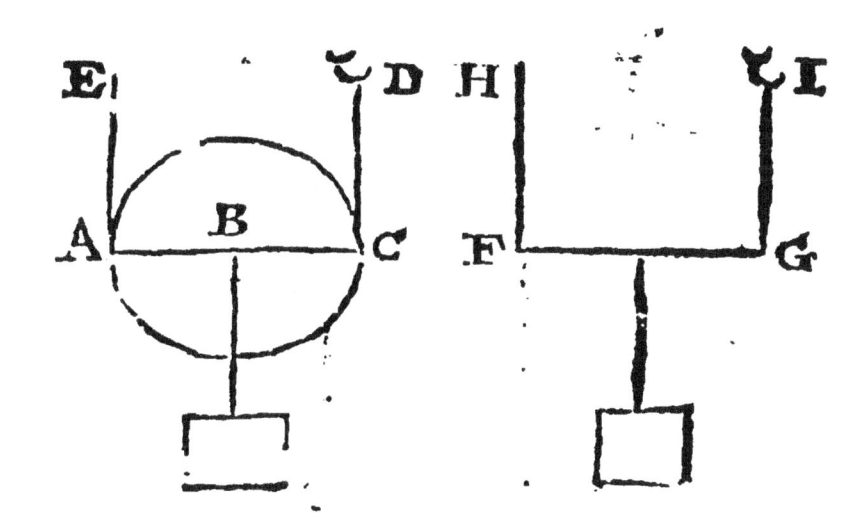

Let *AC*, represent the Diameter of a lower Pulley, on whose center at *B*, the weight is fastned, one end of the cord being tyed to a hook at *D*. Now it is evident, that half the weight is sustained at *D*, so that there is but the other half left to be

sustained

sustained by the power at *E*. It being all one as if the weight were tyed unto the middle of the ballance *F G*, whose ends were upheld by two several strings, *F H*, and *G I*.

And this same subduple proportion will still remain, tho' we suppose an upper Pulley joyned to the lower, as in these two other figures.

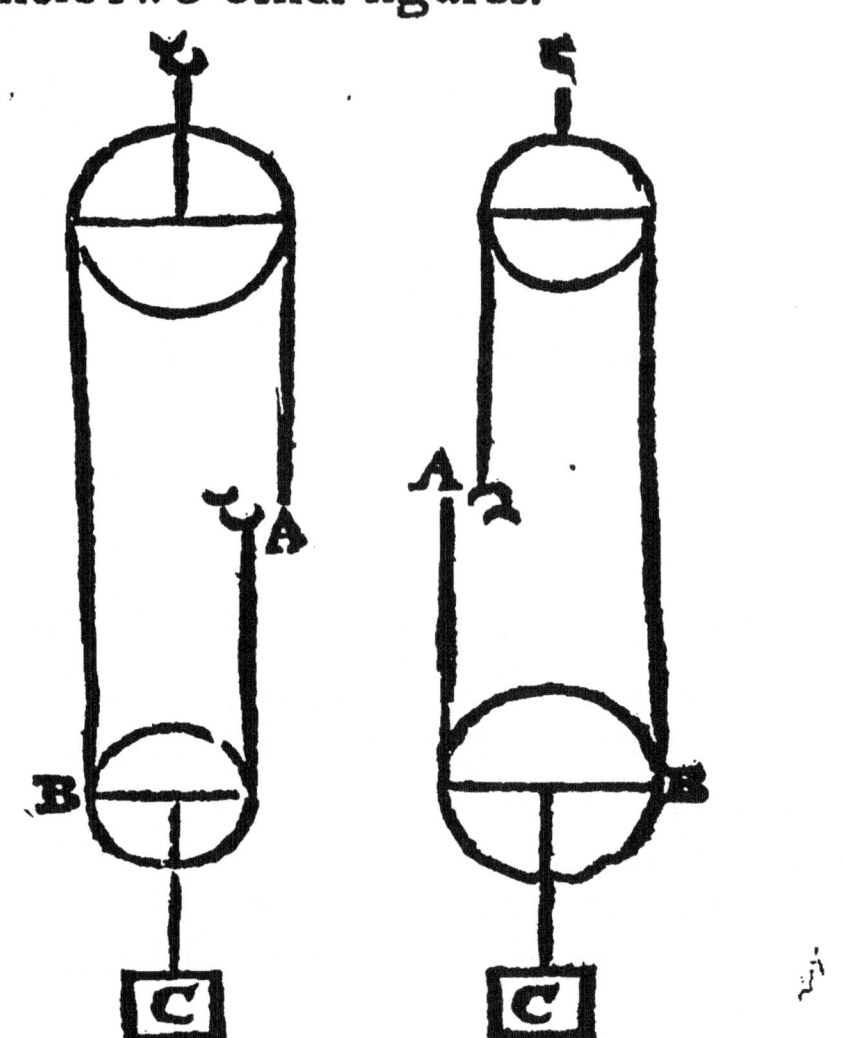

Cap. 7. *Mechanical Powers.*

Where the power at *A*, is equal to the weight at *B* : Now the weight at *B*, being but half the ponderosity *C*, therefore the power at *A*, notwithstanding the addition of the upper rundle, must be equivalent to half the weight; and as the upper Pulley alone doth not abate any thing of the weight, so neither being joined with the lower, and the same subduple difference betwixt the power and the weight, which is caused by the lower Pulley alone, doth still remain unaltered, though there be an upper Pulley added unto it.

Now as one of these under Pulleys doth abate half of that heaviness which the weight hath in it self, and cause the power to be in a subduple proportion unto it; so two of them do abate half of that which remains, and cause a subquadruple proportion, betwixt the weight and the power; three of them a subsextuple, four a suboctuple : and so for five, or six, or as many as shall be required, they will all of them diminish

the

the weight according to this proportion.

Suppose the weight in it self to be 1200 pound, the applying unto it one of these lower Pulleys, will make it but as 600, two of them as 300, three of them as 150. &c.

But now, if we conceive the first part of the string to be fastened unto the lower Pulley, as in this other figure at F;

Cap. 7. *Mechanical Powers.*

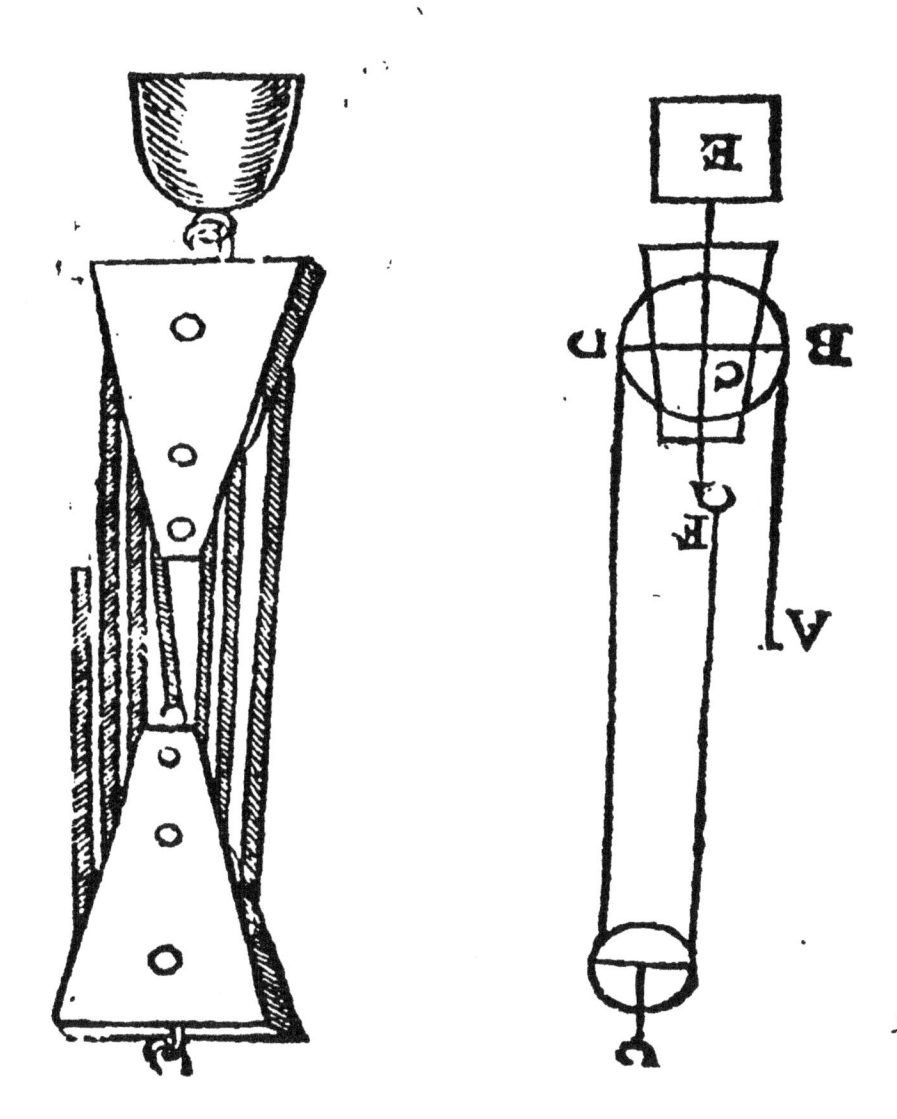

then the power at *A* will be in a subtriple proportion to the weight *E*, because the heaviness would be then equally divided unto the three points of the lower Diameter *B C D*, each

of

of them supporting a like share of the burden. If unto this lower Pulley there were added another, then the power would be unto the weight in a subquintuple proportion. If a third, a subseptuple, and so of the rest. For we must note, that the cords in this instrument are as so many powers, and the rundles as so many leavers, or ballances.

Hence it is easie to conceive, how the strength of the power may be proportioned according to any such degree, as shall be required; and how any weight given, may be moved by any power given.

'Tis not material to the force of this instrument, whether the rundles of it be big or little, if they be made equal to one another in their several orders; but it is most convenient, that the upper should each of them increase as they are higher, and the other as they are lower, because by this means the cords will be kept from tangling.

These Pulleys may be multiplied ac-

Cap. 7. *Mechanical Powers.* 51

according to sundry different situations, not only when they are subordinate, as in the former examples, but also when they are placed collaterally.

From the former grounds it is easie to contrive a ladder, by which a man may pull himself up unto any height; For the performance of this, there is required only an upper and a lower rundle:

To the uppermost of these at *A*, there should be fastned a sharp grapple or cramp of iron, which may be apt to take hold of any place where it lights. This part being first cast up and fastned, and the staff *D E*, at the nether end, being put betwixt the legs, so that a man may sit upon the other *B C*, and take hold of the cord at *F*, it is evident that the weight of the person at *E*, will be but equal to half so much strength at *F*, so that a man may easily pull himself up to the place required, by leaning but little more th n half of his own weight on the string *F*. Or if the Pulleys be multiplied, this experiment may then be wrought with less labour.

CAP. VIII.

Of *the Wedge*.

THE fift Mechanical faculty is the Wedge, which is a known instrument, commonly us'd in the cleaving

Cap. 8. *Mechanical Powers.*

ving of wood. The efficacy and great strength of it may be resolved unto these two particulars:

1. The form of it.
2. The manner whereby the power is impressed upon it, which is by the force of blows.

1. The form of it represents (as it were) two Leavers.

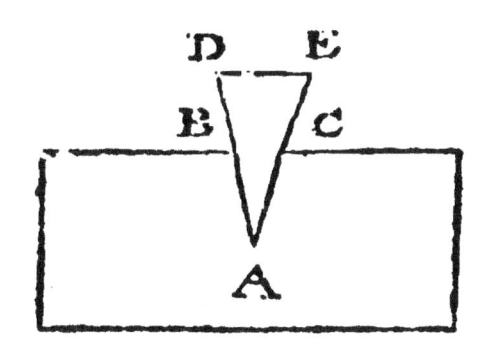

Each side AD, and AE, being one, the points BC, being instead of several props or fulciments; the weight to be moved at A, and the power that should move it, being applied to the top DE, by the force of some stroke or blow, as *Aristotle* hath explained the several parts of this faculty. But now, because this instrument may be so used, that the

Mechan. c. 3.

point of it shall not touch the body to be moved, as in these other figures:

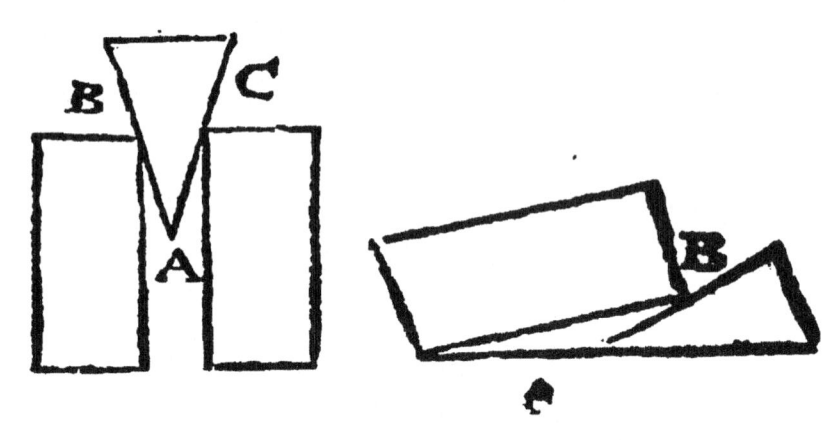

Therefore *Vbaldus* hath more exactly applied the several parts of it according to this form, that the point *A* should be as the common fulciment, in which both the sides do meet, and (as it were) uphold one another; the points *B* and *C*, representing that part of the Leavers where the weight is placed.

It is a general rule, That the more acute the angles of these wedges are, by so much more easie will their motion be; the force being more easily impressed, and the space wherein the body is moved, being so much the less.

The

Cap. 8. *Mechanical Powers.*

The second particular whereby this faculty hath its force, is the *manner* whereby the power is imprest upon it, which is by a stroke or blow; the efficacy of which doth much exceed any other strength. For though we suppose a wedge being laid on a peice of timber, to be pressed down with never so great a weight; nay, though we should apply unto it the power of those other Mechanical engines, the Pulley, Screw, &c. yet the effect would be scarce considerable, in comparison to that of a blow. The true reason of which, is one of the greatest subtilties in nature; nor is it fully rendred by any of those who have undertaken the resolution of it. *Aristotle*, *Cardan*, and *Scaliger*, do generally ascribe it unto the swiftness of that motion; But there seems to be something more in the matter than so; for otherwise it would follow, that the quick stroke of a light hammer, should be of greater efficacy, than any softer and more gentle striking of a great sledge.

Mechan. c. 13. Subt. l. 17 Exercit. 331.

sledge. Or according to this, how should it come to pass, that the force of an arrow or bullet discharged near at hand (when the impression of that violence, whereby they are carried, is most fresh, and so in probability the motion at its swiftest) is yet notwithstanding, much less than it would be at a greater distance? There is therefore further considerable, the quality of that instrument by which this motion is given, and also the conveniency of distance through which it passes.

Unto this faculty is usually reduced the force of files, saws, hatchets, &c. which are, as it were, but so many wedges fastned unto a *Vectis* or Leaver.

CAP. IX.
Of the SCREW.

THat which is usually recited for the sixth and last Mechanick faculty, is the Screw, which is described to be a kind of wedge that is multiplied

Cap. 9. *Mechanical Powers.*

plied or continued by a helical revolution about a Cylinder, receiving its motion not from any stroke, but from a Vectis at one end of it. It is usually distinguished into two several kinds: the male, which is meant in the former description; and the female, which is of a concave superficies.

Pappus. Collect. Mathemat. lib. 8.

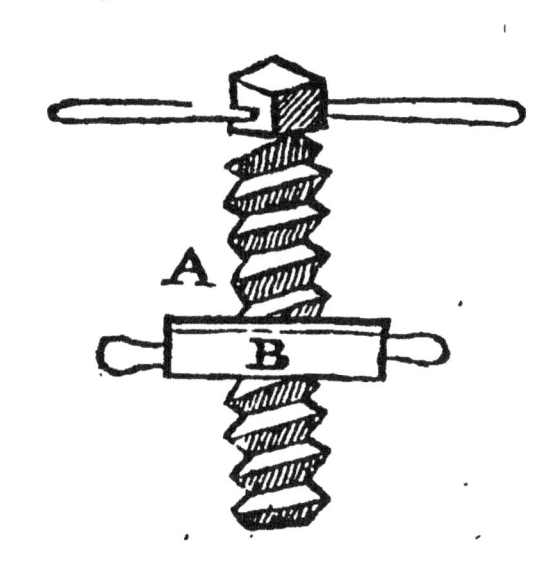

The former is noted in the figure with the letter *A*, the other with *B*.

Aristotle himself doth not so much as mention this instrument, which yet notwithstanding is of greater force and subtilty, than any of the rest. It is chiefly applied to the squeezing or pressing of things downwards,

wards, as in the Presses for Printing, for wine, oyl, and extracting the juice from other fruits, in the performance of which, the strength of one man may be of greater force, than the weight of a heavy mountain: It is likewise used for the elevating or lifting up of weights.

The advantage of this faculty above the rest, doth mainly consist in this: the other instruments do require so much strength for the supporting of the weight to be moved, as may be equal unto it, besides that other super-added power whereby it is out-weighed and moved; so that in the operations by these, a man does always spend himself in a continued labour.

Thus (for example) a weight that is lifted up by a Wheel or Pulley, will of it self descend, if there be not an equal power to sustain it. But now in the composure of a Screw, this inconvenience is perfectly remedied; for so much force as is communicated unto this faculty, from the power

Cap. 9. *Mechanical Powers.*

power that is applied unto it, is still retained by the very frame and nature of the instrument it self; since the motion of it cannot possibly return, but from the very same place where it first began. Whence it comes to pass, that any weight lifted up, with the assistance of this engine, may likewise be sustained by it, without the help of any external power, and cannot again descend unto its former place, unless the handle of the Screw (where the motion first began) be turned back: so that all the strength of the power, may be employed in the motion of the weight, and none spent in the sustaining of it.

The chief inconvenience of this instrument is, that in a short space it will be screwed unto its full length, and then it cannot be of any further use for the continuance of the motion, unless it be returned back, and undone again as at the first. But this is usually remedied by another invention, commonly styled a *perpetual*

tual Screw, which hath the *motion* of a *Wheel*, and the *force* of a *Screw*, being both infinite.

For the compofure of which, inftead of the female, or concave fcrew, there muft be a little Wheel, with fome notches in it, equivalent to teeth, by which the other may take hold of it, and turn it round, as in thefe other figures.

It is ufed in fome Watches.

This latter engine does fo far exceed all other contrivances to this purpofe, that it may juftly feem a wonder why it is not of as common ufe use in these times and places, as any of the rest.

CAP. X.

An enquiry into the magnificent works of the Ancients, which much exceeding our later times, may seem to infer a decay in these Mechanical Arts.

THus have I briefly treated concerning the general principles of Mechanicks, together with the distinct proportions betwixt the weight and the power in each several faculty of it; Whence it is easie to conceive the truth and ground of those famous ancient monuments, which seem almost incredible to these following ages. And because many of them recorded by Antiquity, were of such vast labour and magnificence, and so mightily disproportionable to humane strength, it shall not therefore be impertinent unto the purpose I aim at, for to specifie some

of

of the most remarkable amongst them, and to enquire into the means and occasion upon which they were first attempted.

Amongst the *Ægyptians*, we read of divers Pyramids, of so vast a magnitude, as time it self in the space of so many hundred years hath not yet devoured. *Herodotus* mentions one of them, erected by *Cleopes* an Ægyptian King, wherein there was not any one stone less than 30 foot long, all of them being fetched from *Arabia*. And not much after, the same Author relates, how *Amasis* another *Ægyptian*, made himself a house of one entire stone, which was 21 cubits long, 14 broad, and 8 cubits high. The same *Amasis* is reported to have made the statue of a *Sphinx*, or *Ægyptian* Cat, all of one single stone, whose length was 143 foot, its height 62 foot, the compass of this statue's head containing 102 foot. In one of the *Ægyptian* Temples consecrated to *Jupiter*, there is related to be an Obelisk, consisting of 4 Smaragds

L. 2. c. 175.

Plin. l. 36. ca. 12.

Plin. l. 37. cap. 5.

or

or Emeralds; the whole is 40 cubits high, 4 cubits broad at the bottom, and two at the top. *Sesostris* the King of Ægypt, in a Temple at *Memphis*, dedicated to *Vulcan*, is reported to have erected two statues, one for himself, the other for his wife, both consisting of two several stones, each of which were 30 cubits high.

Diodo. Sicul. Biblioth. l. 1. Sect. 2.

Amongst the Jews we read in sacred Writ of *Solomon*'s Temple, which for its state and magnificence, might have been justly reckoned amongst the other wonders of the world, wherein besides the great riches of the materials, there were works too of as great labour. Pillars of brass 18 cubits high, and 12 cubits round; great and costly stones for the foundation of it; *Josephus* tells us, that some of them were 40 cubits, others 45 cubits long. And in the same Chapter he mentions the three famous Towers built by *Herod*, wherein every stone being of white marble, was 20 cubits long, 10 broad, and 5 high. And which was the greatest

1 Kings 2. 15. cap. 5. v. 17.

De bello Juda. l. 6. c. 6.

won-

wonder, the old wall it self was situated on a steep rising ground, and yet the hills upon it, on the tops of which these Towers were placed, were about 30 cubits high, that 'tis scarce imaginable by what strength so many stones of such great magnitude should be conveyed to so high a place.

Plin. l. 36. c. 14. Paucirol. Deperd. Tit. 32.

Amongst the *Grecians* we read of the *Ephesian* Temple dedicated to *Diana*, wherein there were 127 columns, made of so many several stones, each of them 60 foot high, being all taken out of the quarries in *Asia*. 'Tis storied also of the brazen *Colossus*, or great Statue in the Island of *Rhodes*, that it was 70 cubits high, The thumbs of it being so big that no man could grasp one of them about with both his arms; when it stood upright, a ship might have passed betwixt the legs of it, with all its sails fully displayed; being thrown down by an earth-quake, the brass of it did load 900 Camels. But above all ancient designs to this purpose, that would have been most wonder-

Plin. l. 34. c. 3.

wonderful, which a Grecian Architect did propound unto *Alexander*, to cut the Mountain *Athos* into the form of a statue, which in his right hand should hold a Town capable of ten thousand men, and in his left a Vessel to receive all the water that flowed from the several springs in the Mountain. But whether *Alexander* in his ambition did fear that such an Idol should have more honour than he himself, or whether in his good husbandry, he thought that such a *Microcosm* (if I may so style it) would have cost him almost as much as the conquering of this great world, or what ever else was the reason, he refused to attempt it.

Vitruv. Archit. l. 2.

Amongst the *Romans* we read of a brazen *Colossus*, made at the command and charges of *Nero*, which was 120 foot high; *Martial* calls it *Sydereus*, or starry

Suet. Ner.

Hic ubi Sydereus proprius vidit astra Colossus. And it is storied of M. *Curio*, that he erected two *Theatres* sufficiently

Pancirol Deperd. Tit. 18.

ently capacious of people, contrived movable upon certain hinges; Sometimes there were several plays and shows in each of them, neither being any disturbance to the other; and sometimes they were both turned about, with the people in them, and the ends meeting together, did make a perfect *Amphitheater*: so that the spectators which were in either of them, might joyntly behold the same spectacles.

De Tit. 31.

There were besides at *Rome* sundry *Obelisks*, made of so many intire stones, some of them 40, some 80, and others 90 cubits high. The chief of them were brought out of *Ægypt*, where they were dug out of divers quaries, and being wrought into form, were afterward (not without incredible labour, and infinite charges) conveyed unto *Rome*. In the year 1586, there was erected an old *Obelisk*, which had been formerly dedicated unto the memory of *Julius Cæsar*. It was one solid stone, being an Ophite or kind of spotted Marble. The height of it was 107 foot, the breadth of it

at

Cap. 10. *Mechanical Powers.*

at the bottom was 12 foot, at the top 8. Its whole weight is reckoned to be 956148 pounds, besides the heaviness of all those instruments that were used about it, which (as it is thought) could not amount to less then 1042824 pounds. It was transplaced at the charges of Pope *Sixtus* the fifth, from the left side of the *Vatican*, unto a more eminent place about a hundred foot off, where now it stands. The moving of this *Obelisk* is celebrated by the writings of above 56 several Authors, (saith *Monantholius*) all of them mentioning it, not without much wonder and praise. Now if it seem so strange and glorious an attempt to move this *Obelisk* for so little a space, what then may we think of the carriage of it out of *Egypt*, and divers other far greater works performed by Antiquity? This may seem to infer, that these Mechanical arts are now lost, and decayed amongst the many other ruins of time; which yet notwithstanding cannot be granted, without much ingratitude

Comment. in Mechan. Arist. c. 19.

tude to those learned men, whose labours in this kind we enjoy, and may justly boast of. And therefore for our better understanding of these particulars, it will not be amiss to enquire both *why*, and *how*, such works should be perform'd in those former and ruder ages, which *are not*, and (as it should seem) *cannot* be effected in these later and more learned times. In the examination of which, we shall find, that it is not the want of Art that disables us for them, since these Mechanical discoveries are altogether as perfect, and (I think) much more exact now, than they were heretofore; but it is, because we have not either the same *motives* to attempt such works, or the same *means* to effect them as the Ancients had.

C A P.

CAP. XI.

That the Ancients had divers motives and means for such vast magnificent works, which we have not.

THE *motives* by which they were excited to such magnificent attempts, we may conceive to be chiefly three.

$$\begin{cases} Religion. \\ Policy. \\ Ambition. \end{cases}$$

1. *Religion.* Hence was it that most of these stately buildings were intended for some sacred use, being either Temples or * Tombs, all of them dedicated to some of their Deities. It was an in-bred principle in those ancient Heathen, that they could not chuse but merit very much by being liberal in their outward services. And therefore we read of *Cræsus*, that being overcome in a battel, and taken by *Cyrus*, he did revile the Gods of ingratitude, because they had no better care of him, who had so frequently adored

*As Pyramids, Obelisks.

Herodot. l. 1.

adored them with costly oblations. And as they did conceive themselves bound to part with their lives in defence of their Religion, so likewise to employ their utmost power and estate, about any such design which might promote or advance it. Whereas now, the generality of men, especially the wisest sort amongst them, are in this respect of another opinion, counting such great and immense labours to be at the best but glorious vanities. The temple of *Solomon* indeed was to be a type, and therefore it was necessary that it should be so extraordinarily magnificent, otherwise perhaps a much cheaper structure might have been as commendable and serviceable.

2. *Policy*, that by this means they might find out imployment for the people, who of themselves being not much civilized, might by idleness quickly grow to such a rudeness and barbarism, as not to be bounded within any laws of government. Again, by this means the riches of the Kingdom

dom did not lye idlely in their Kings Treasuries, but was always in motion, which could not but be a great advantage and improvement to the Commonwealth. And perhaps some of them feared, lest if they should leave too much money unto their successors, it might be an occasion to insnare them in such idle and vain courses as would ruin their Kingdoms. Whereas in these later ages none of all these politick incitements can be of any force, because now there is imployment enough for all, and money little enough for every one.

3. *Ambition* to be known unto posterity; and hence likewise arose that incredible labour and care they bestowed to leave such monuments behind them, as might * *continue for ever*, and make them famous unto all after ages: This was the reason of *Absaloms* Pillar spoken of in Scripture, *to keep his name in remembrance.* And doubtless this too was the end which many others of the Ancients have aimed at, in those (as they thought)

* Psal. 49. 21.

2 Sam. 18. 18.

thought) everlasting buildings.

But now these later ages are much more active and stirring: so that every ambitious man may find so much business for the present, that he shall scarce have any leisure to trouble himself about the future. And therefore in all these respects, there is a great disproportion betwixt the incitements of those former and these later times unto such magnificent attempts.

Again, as they differ much in their *motives* unto them, so likewise in the means of effecting them.

There was formerly more leisure and opportunity, both for the great men to undertake such works, and for the people to perfect them. Those past ages were more quiet and peaceable, the Princes rather wanting imployment, than being over-prest with it, and therefore were willing to make choice of such great designs, about which to busie themselves: whereas now the world is grown more politick, and therefore more trouble-

Cap. 11. *Mechanical Powers.*

troublesome, every great man having other private and necessary business about which to employ both his time and means. And so likewise for the common people, who then living more wildly, without being confined to particular trades and professions, might be more easily collected about such famous Employments; whereas now, if a Prince have any occasion for an Army, it is very hard for him to raise so great a multitude, as were usually imployed about these magnificent buildings. We read of 360000 men that were busied for twenty years in making one of the *Egyptian* Pyramids. And *Herodotus* tels us of 1000000 men who were as long in building another of them. About the carriage of one stone for *Amasis*, the distance of twenty days journey, there was for three years together employed 2000 chosen men, Governours, besides many other under-labourers. 'Twas the opinion of * *Josephus* and *Nazianzen*, that these Pyramids were built by *Joseph* for Granaries against the

Lib. 2.

* Antiq. l. 2. c. 5.

years

years of famine. Others think that the brick made by the children of *Ifrael*, was imployed about the framing of them, because we read that the Tower of *Babel* did confift of brick or artificial ftone, *Gen.* 11. 3. And if thefe were the labourers that were bufied about them, 'tis no wonder though they were of fo vaft a magnitude; for we read that the children of *Ifrael* at their coming out of *Egypt*, were numbred to be fix hundred thoufand, and three thoufand, and five hundred and fifty men, *Num.* 1. 46. fo many handfuls of earth would almoft make a mountain, and therefore we may eafily believe that fo great a multitude in fo long a fpace as their bondage lafted, for above four hundred years, might well enough accomplifh fuch vaft defigns.

In the building of *Solomon*'s Temple, there were threefcore and ten thoufand that bare burdens, and fourfcore thoufand hewers in the mountains, 1 *Kings* 5. 15.

The *Ephefian* Temple was built by all

Cap. 11. *Mechanical Powers.*

all *Asia* joyning together, the 127 pillars were made by so many Kings according to their several successions; the whole work being not finished under the space of Two hundred and fifteen years. Whereas the transplacing of that Obelisk at *Rome*, by *Sixtus* the fifth, (spoken of before) was done in some few days by five or six hundred men; and as the work was much less than many other recorded by Antiquity; so the means by which it was wrought, was yet far less in this respect than what is related of them.

2. The abundance of wealth which was then ingrossed in the possession of some few particular persons, being now diffused amongst a far greater number. There is now a greater equality amongst mankind; and the flourishing of Arts and Sciences hath so stirred up the sparks of mens natural nobility, and made them of such active and industrious spirits, as to free themselves in a great measure, from that slavery, which those former and

wilder

wilder Nations were subjected unto.

In building one of the Pyramids, there was expended for the maintenance of the labourers with Radish and Onyons, no less than eighteen hundred talents, which is reckoned to amount unto 1880000 Crowns, or thereabouts. And considering the cheapness of these things in those times and places, so much money might go farther than a sum ten times greater could do in the maintenance of so many now.

In *Solomon*'s Temple we know how the extraordinary riches of that King, the general flourishing of the whole State, and the liberality of the people did jointly concur to the building of the Temple. *Pecuniarum copia, & populi largitus, majora dictu conabatur*, (saith *Josephus*). The *Rhodian* Colossus is reported to have cost three hundred talents the making. And so were all those other famous Monuments of proportionable expence.

Pancirollus speaking of those Theatres that were erected at the charges of

De bell. Jud. l. 6. cap. 6.

of some private *Roman* Citizens, saith thus, *Nostro hoc sæculo vel Rex satis haberet quod ageret ædificio ejusmodi erigendo*: and a little after upon the like occasion, *Res mehercule miraculosa, quæ nostris temporibus vix à potentissimo aliquo rege possit exhiberi.*

Deperd. Tit. 18.

3. Add unto the two former considerations that exact *care* and indefatigable *industry* which they bestowed in the raising of those structures: These being the chief and only designs on which many of them did employ all their best thoughts and utmost endeavours. *Cleopes* an *Egyptian* King is reported to have been so desirous to finish one of the Pyramids, that having spent all about it he was worth, or could possibly procure, he was forced at last to prostitute his own daughter for necessary maintenance. And we read of *Ramises* another King of *Egypt*, how that he was so careful to erect an Obelisk, about which he had employed 20000 men, that when he feared lest through the negligence of the artificers, or weakness of the engine,

Plin. l. 36. c. 9.

gine, the stone might fall and break, he tyed his own son to the top of it, that so the care of his safety might make the workmen more circumspect in their business. And what strange matters may be effected by the meer diligence and labour of great multitudes, we may easily discern from the wild *Indians*, who having not the art or advantage of Engines, did yet by their unwearied industry remove stones of an incredible greatness. *Acosta* relates, that he himself measured one at *Tiaguanaco*, which was thirty eight foot long, eighteen broad, and six thick; and he affirms, that in their stateliest Edifices, there were many other of much vaster magnitude.

Histor. Ind. l. 6. c. 14.

From all which considerations it may appear, That the strangeness of those ancient monuments above any that are now effected, does not necessarily infer any defect of Art in these later Ages. And I conceive, it were as easie to demonstrate the Mechanical Arts in these times to be so far beyond the knowledge of former ages,

ages, that had we but the same means as the Ancients had, we might effect far greater matters than any they attempted, and that too in a shorter space, and with less labour.

CAP. XII.

Concerning the force of the Mechanick faculties, particularly the Ballance and Leaver. How they may be contrived to move the whole world, or any other conceivable weight.

ALL these magnificent works of the Ancients before specified, are scarce considerable in respect of Art, if we compare them with the famous speeches and acts of *Archimedes*: Of whom it is reported, that he was frequently wont to say, how that he could move, *Datum pondus cum datâ potentiâ*, the greatest conceivable weight, with the least conceivable power: and that if he did but know where to stand and fasten his instrument, he could move the world, all this

this great Globe of sea and land; which *promises*, though they were altogether above the vulgar apprehension or belief, yet because his *acts* were somewhat answerable thereunto, therefore the King of *Syracuse* did enact a law whereby every man was bound to believe what ever *Archimedes* would affirm.

'Tis easie to demonstrate the Geometrical truth of those strange assertions, by examining them according to each of the forenamed *Mechanick* faculties, every one of which is of infinite power.

To begin with the two first of them, the Ballance and the Leaver, (which I here joyn together, because the proportions of both are wholly alike) 'tis certain, though there should be the greatest imaginable weight, and the least imaginable power, (suppose the whole world, and the strength of one man or infant) yet if we conceive the same disproportion betwixt their several distances in the former faculties from the fulciment or center of gravity,

Cap. 12. *Mechanical Powers.*

vity, they would both equiponderate. And if the distance of the power from the center, in comparison to the distance of the weight, were but any thing more than the heaviness of the weight is in respect of the power, it may then be evident from the former principles, that the power would be of greater force than the weight, and consequently able to move it.

Thus if we suppose this great globe at *A*, to
con-

contain 240000000000000000000000 pounds, allowing a hundred pound for each cubical foot in it, (as *Stevinius* hath calculated) yet a man or child at *D*, whose strength perhaps is but equivalent to one hundred, or ten pounds weight, may be able to outweigh and move it, if there be but a little greater disproportion betwixt the two distances *C D*, and *C B*, than there is betwixt the heaviness of the weight, and the strength of the power; that is, if the distance *C D*, unto the other distance *C B*, be any thing more than 240000000000000000000000 unto 100 or 10, every ordinary instrument doth include all these parts *really*, though not sensibly distinguished.

Static. l.3. prop. 10.

Under this latter faculty I did before mention that engine by which *Archimedes* drew up the *Roman* Ships at the siege of *Syracuse*. This is usually styled *Tollenon*, being of the same form with that which is commonly used by Brewers and Dyers, for the drawing of water. It consists of two posts,

Lipsius Poliorcet. l. 1. Dialog. 6.

Cap. 12. *Mechanical Powers.*

posts, the one fastned perpendicularly in the ground, the other being jointed on cross to the top of it. At the end he fastned a strong hook or grapple of iron, which being let over the Wall, to the River, he would thereby take hold of the Ships, as they passed under, and afterwards by applying some weight, or perhaps the force of Screws to the other end, he would thereby lift them into the open air, where having swinged them up and down till he had shaken out the men and goods that were in them, he would then dash the Vessels against the rocks, or drown them in their sudden fall: insomuch that *Marcellus*, the *Roman* General, was wont to say, τ̓ μὲν ναυσὶν αὐτῷ κυαδίζειν ἐκ θαλάτ‍της Ἀρχιμήδην, That *Archimedes* made use of his Ships, instead of Buckets, to draw water with. *Plutarch in his life.*

This faculty will be of the same force, not only when it is continued in one, but also when it is multiplied in divers instruments, as may be conceived in this other form, which I do not mention as if it could be serviceable for any motion (since the space by which the weight would be moved, will be so little as not to fall under sense) but only for the better explication of this Mechanick principle, and for the right understanding of that force arising from multiplication in the other faculties, which do all depend upon this. The Wheel, and Pulley, and Screw, being but as so many Leavers of a circular form and motion, whose strength may therefore be continued to a greater space.

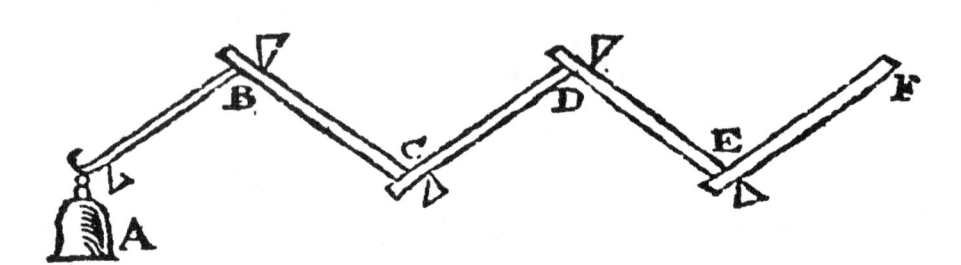

Imagine the weight *A* to be an hundred thousand pounds, and the distance of that point, wherein every Leaver touches either the weight or one another, from the point where they touch the prop, to be but one such

Cap. 12. *Mechanical Powers.* 85

such part, whereof the remainder contains ten; then according to the former grounds 10000 at *B*, will equiponderate to *A*, which is 100000, so that the second Leaver hath but 10000 pounds to move. Now because this observes the same proportions with the other in the distances of its several points, therefore 1000 pounds at *C*, will be of equal weight to the former. And the weight at *C*, being but as a thousand pound, that which is but as a hundred at *D*, will be answerable unto it; and so still in the same proportion, that which is but 10 at *E*, will be equal to 100 at *D*; and that which is but one pound at F, will also be equal to ten at *E*. Whence it is manifest, that 1 pound at *F*, is equal to 100000 at *A*; and the weight must always be diminished in the same proportion as ten to one, because in the multiplication of these Leavers, the distance of the point, where the instrument touches the weight, from that where it touches the prop, is but as one such

G 3 part

part whereof the remainder contains ten. But now if we imagine it to be as the thousandth part, then must the weight be diminish'd according to this proportion; and then in the same multiplication of Leavers, 1 *l.* will be equal to 1000 000 000 000 000 pounds ; so that though we suppose the weight to be never so heavy, yet let the disproportion of distances be greater, or the Leavers more, and any little power may move it.

CAP. XIII.

Of the Wheel, by multiplication of which it is easie to move any imaginable weight.

THE Wheel, or *axis in peritrochio*, was before demonstrated to be of equivalent force with the former faculties. If we conceive the same difference betwixt the Semidiameter of the wheels or spokes *A C*, and the Semidiameter of the axis *A B*, as there is betwixt the weight of the world,

See the figure, cap. 6. p. 38.

Cap. 13. *Mechanical Powers.*

and the strength of a man, it may then be evident, that this strength of one man, by the help of such an instrument, will equiponderate to the weight of the whole world. And if the Semidiameter of the wheel AC, be but any thing more in respect of the Semidiameter of the axis AB, then the weight of the world supposed at D, is in comparison to the strength of a man at C; it may then be manifest from the same grounds, that this strength will be of so much greater force than the weight, and consequently able to move it.

The force of this faculty may be more conveniently understood and used by the multiplication of several wheels, together with nuts belonging unto each of them; as it may be easily experimented in the ordinary Jacks that are used for the roasting of meat, which commonly consist but of three wheels; and yet if we suppose a man tyed in the place of the weight, it were easie by a single hair fastned unto the fly or ballance of the Jack,

An engine of many wheels is commonly called, Glossocomus.

How to pull a man above ground with a single hair.

88   *Archimedes; or,* Lib. I.

Jack, to draw him up from the ground, as will be evident from this following figure.

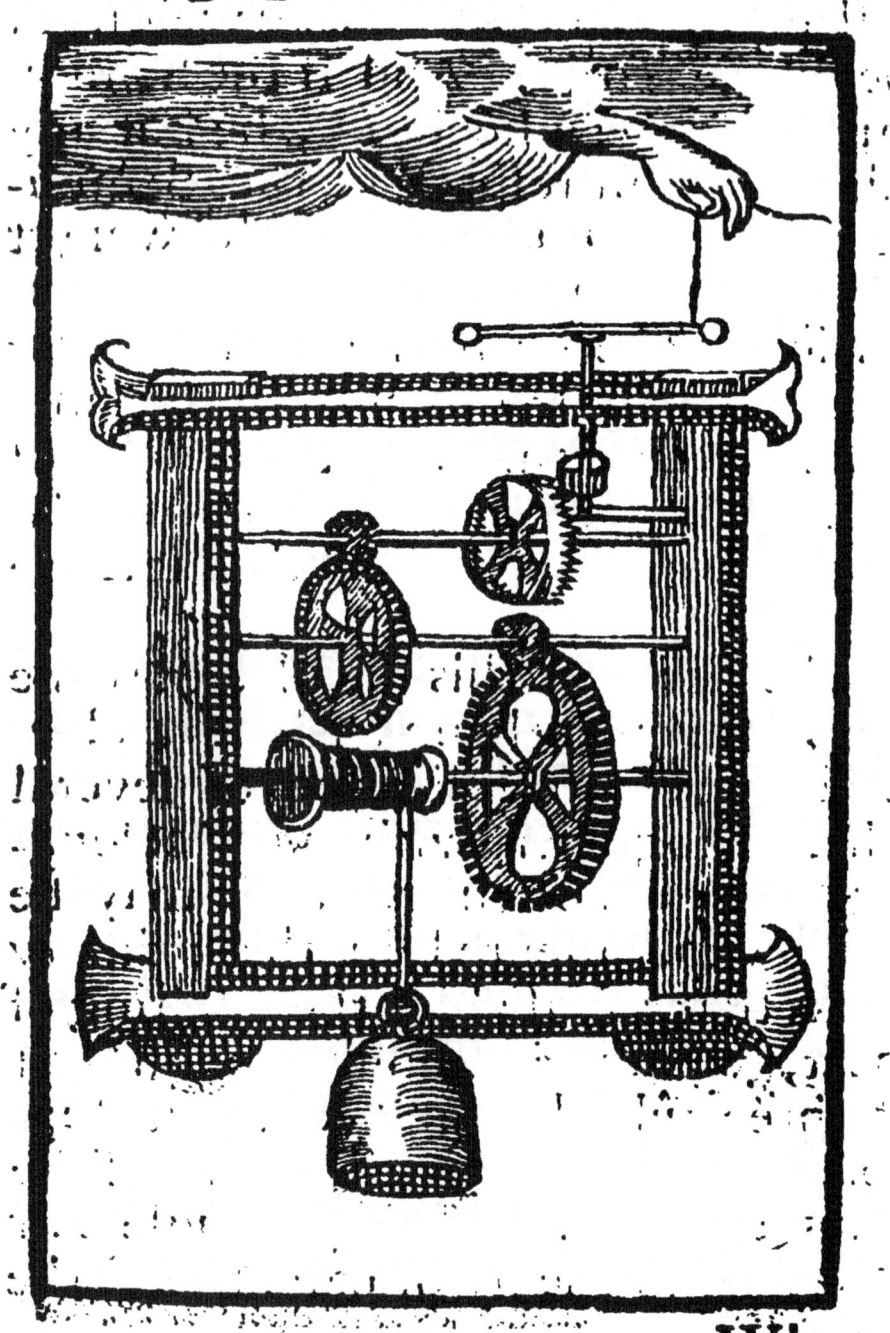

Where

Cap. 13. Mechanical Powers. 89

Where suppose the length of the flye or ballance in comparison to the breadth of its axis, to be as 10 to one, and so for the three other wheels in respect of the nuts that belong unto them; (though this difference be oftentimes less, as we may well allow it to be) withall suppose the weight (or a man tyed in the place of it) to be a hundred pounds: I say, according to this supposition, it is evident that the power at the ballance, which shall be equal to the weight, need be but as 1 to 10000. For the first axis is concieved to be but as the tenth part of its wheel; and therefore though the weight in it self be as 10000, yet unto a power that hath this advantage, it is but as 1000, and therefore this thousand unto the like power at the second wheel, will be but as 100, and this 100 at the third but as 10; and lastly, this ten at the ballance but as one. But the weight was before supposed to be 100, which to the first wheel will be but 10, to the second as one, to the third as a decimal,

mal, or one tenth, to the sails as one hundredth part: so that if the hair be but strong enough to lift $\frac{1}{10000}$, that is one ten thousandth part of a man, or (which is all one) one hundreth part of a pound, it may as well serve by the help of this Instrument for the drawing of him up. And though there be not altogether so great a disproportion betwixt the several parts of a Jack, (as in many perhaps there is not); and though a man may be heavier than is here supposed; yet 'tis with all considerable, that the strength of a hair is able to bear much more than the hundredth part of a pound.

<small>Coment. in Gen. c. 1. v. 10. art. 6. De viribus motricib. Theor. 16.</small>

Upon this ground *Mersennus* tells us out of *Solomon de Cavet*, that if there were an engine of 12 wheels each of them with teeth, as also the axes or nuts that belong unto them, if the Diameter of these wheels were unto each *axis*, as a hundred to one; and if we suppose these wheels to be so placed, that the teeth of the one might take hold of the axis that belongs unto the next; and that the axis

of

of the handle may turn the first wheel, and the weight be tyed unto the axis of the last; with such an engine as this, saith he, a child (if he could stand any where without this earth) might with much ease move it towards him.

For according to the former supposition, that this Globe of sea and land, did contain as many hundred pounds, as it doth cubical feet, *viz.* 2400000000000000000000000, it may be evident that any strength, whose force is but equivalent to 3 pounds, will by such an engine be able to move it.

Of this kind was that engine so highly extolled by *Stevinius*, which he calls *Pancration*, or *Omnipotent*, preferring it before the inventions of *Archimedes*. It consisted of wheels and nuts, as that before specified is supposed. Hither also should be referred the force of racks, which serve for bending of the strongest bows, as also that little pocket-engine wherewith a man may break or wrench open

De Statica proxi.

Ramilli. Fig. 160.

pen any door, together with divers the like instruments in common use.

CAP. XIV.

Concerning the infinite strength of Wheels, Pulleys, and Screws. That it is possible by the multiplication of these, to pull up any Oak by the roots with a hair, lift it up with a straw, or blow it up with ones breath, or to perform the greatest labour with the least power.

FRom what hath been before delivered concerning the nature of the Pulley, it is easie to understand, how this faculty also may be proportioned betwixt any weight, and any power, as being likewise of infinite strength.

'Tis reported of *Archimedes*, that with an engine of Pulleys, to which he applyed only his left hand, he lifted up * 5000 bushels of Corn at once, and drew a ship with all its lading

* 7000 saith *Zetzes* Chiliad. 2. Hist. 35.

ding upon dry land. This engine *Zetzes* calls *Trispatum*, or *Trispastum*, which signifies only a threefold Pulley. But herein he doth evidently mistake; for 'tis not possible that this alone should serve for the motion of so great a weight, because such an engine can but make a subsextuple, or at most a subseptuple proportion betwixt the weight and power, which is much too little to reconcile the strength of a man unto so much heaviness. Therefore *Ubaldus* doth more properly style it *Polyspaston*, or an instrument of many Pulleys: How many, were easie to find out, if we did exactly know the weight of those ancient measures; supposing them to be the same with our bushel in *England*, which contains 64 pints or pounds, the whole would amount to 320000 pounds, half of which would be lightned by the help of one Pulley, three quarters by two Pulleys, and so onward, according to this subduple, subquadruple, and subsextuple proportion: So that if we conceive the strength of

Præf. ad. Mechan.

of the left hand to be equivalent unto 20 or 40 pounds, it is is easie to find out how many Pulleys are required to inable it for the motion of so great a weight.

Comment. in Gen. c. 1. v. 10. art. 6.

Upon this ground *Mersennus* tells us, that any little child with an engine of an hundred double Pulleys, might easily move this great Globe of earth, though it were much heavier than it is. And in reference to this kind of engine (saith *Monantholius*) are we to understand that assertion of *Archimedes* (as he more immediately intended it) concerning the possibility of moving the World.

Præf. ad Mechan. Aristotle.

The Wedg was before demonstrated to be as a double Vectis or Leaver, and therefore it would be needless to explain particularly how this likewise may be contrived of infinite force.

The Screw is capable of multiplication, as well as any of the other faculties, and may perhaps be more serviceable for such great weights, than any of the rest. *Archimedes* his engine

Cap. 14. *Mechanical Powers.*

engine of greatest strength, called *Charistion*, is by some thought to consist of these. *Axis habebat cum infinitis cochleis.* And that other engine of his called *Helix* (mentioned by * *Athenæus*) wherewith he lifted *Hiero's* great ship into the sea, without any other help, is most likely to be framed of perpetual screws, saith *Rivaltus*.

Stevin de Static. prax. See Besson.

*Deiponosophist.l.5. oper.exter. Archimed.

Whence it may evidently appear, that each of these Mechanick faculties are of infinite power, and may be contrived proportionable unto any conceivable weight: And that no natural strength is any way comparable unto these artificial inventions.

'Tis reported of *Sampson*, that he could carry the gates of a City upon his shoulders, and that the strongest bonds were unto him but as flax burnt with fire; and yet his hair being shaved off, all his strength departed from him. We * read of *Milo*, that he could carry an Oxe upon his back, and yet when he tried to tear an Oak asunder,

Judg. 15.

* A. Gel- Noct. Art. l.15. c.16.

der, that was somewhat riven before, having drawn it to its utmost, it suddenly joyned together again, catching his hands in the cleft, and so strongly manacled him, that he became a prey to the wild beasts.

But now by these Mechanical contrivances, it were easie to have made one of *Sampson's* hairs that was shaved off, to have been of more strength than all of them when they were on. By the help of these arts it is possible (as I shall demonstrate) for any man to lift up the greatest Oak by the roots with a straw, to pull it up with a hair, or to blow it up with his breath.

Suppose the roots of an Oak to extend a thousand foot square, (which is almost a quarter of a mile) and forty foot deep, each cubical foot being a hundred pound weight; which though it be much beyond the extension of any tree, or the weight of the earth, the compass of the roots in the ground (according to common opinion) not extending further than the branches of it in the air, and the depth

Cap. 14. Mechanical Powers.

depth of it not above ten foot, beyond which the greatest rain doth not penetrate (saith *Seneca*). *Ego vinearum diligens fossor affirmo nullam pluviam esse tam magnam, quæ terram ultra decem pedes in altitudinem madefaciat.* And because the root must receive its nourishment from the help of showers, therefore it is probable that it doth not go below them. So that (I say) though the proportions supposed do much exceed the real truth, yet it is considerable that some great overplus must be allowed for that labour which there will be in the forcible divulsion or separation of the parts of the earth which are continued.

* Nat. Qu. l. 3. c. 7.

According to this supposition, the work of forcing up the Oak by the roots will be equivalent to the lifting up of 400000000 pound weight, which by the advantage of such an engine, as is here described, may be easily performed with the least conceivable power.

98   *Archimedes; or,*   Lib. I.

Cap. 14. *Mechanical Powers.*

The whole force of this engine doth confist in two double Pulleys, twelve wheels, and a fail. One of thefe Pulleys at the bottome will diminifh half of the weight, fo that it fhall be but as 2000000000, and the other Pulley will abate ¼ three quarters of it; fo that it fhall be but as 1000000000. And becaufe the beginning of the ftring being faftned unto the lower Pulley, makes the power to be in a fubquintuple proportion unto the weight, therefore a power that fhall be as 100000000, that is, a fubquadruple, will be fo much ftronger than the weight, and confequently able to move it. Now fuppofe the breadth of all the axes and nuts, to be unto the Diameters of the wheel as ten to one; and it will then be evident, that to a power at the firft wheel, the weight is but as 100000000. To the fecond as 10000000. To the third as 1000000. To the fourth as 100000. To the fifth as 10000. To the fixth as 1000. To the feventh as 100, To the eighth

See ch. 7.

H 2 as

as 10. To the ninth as 1. To the tenth as $\frac{1}{10}$ one decimal. To the eleventh as $\frac{1}{100}$ To the twelfth as $\frac{1}{1000}$. And the failes yet less. So that if the strength of the straw, or hair, or breath, be but equal to the weight of one thousandth part of a pound, it may be of sufficient force to pull up the Oak.

If in this engine we suppose the disproportion betwixt the wheels and nuts, to be as an hundred to one, then it is very evident, that the same strength of breath, or a hair, or a straw, would be able to move the whole world, as will be easily found by calculation. Let this great Globe of sea and land be imagined (as before) to weigh so many hundred pounds as it contains cubical feet; namely, 2400000000000000000000000 pounds. This will be to the first Pulley, 1200000000000000000000000. To the second less than 600000000000000000000000. But for more easie and convenient reckoning, let it be supposed to be somewhat more, *viz.* 1000000000000000000000000.

This

Cap. 14. *Mechanical Powers.*

This to the first wheel will be but as

	1000000000000000000000.
To the second as	100000000000000000000.
To the third as	1000000000000000000.
To the fourth as	10000000000000000.
To the fifth	100000000000000.
To the sixth	1000000000000.
To the seventh	10000000000.
To the eighth	100000000.
To the ninth	1000000.
To the tenth	10000.
To the eleventh	100.
To the twelfth	1.
To the sails as	$\frac{1}{100}$

So that a power which is much less than the hundredth part of a pound, will be able to move the world.

It were needless to set down any particular explication, how such Mechanical strength may be applyed unto all the kinds of local motion; since this, in it self, is so facile and obvious, that every ordinary Artificer doth sufficiently understand it.

The Species of local violent motion are by *Aristotle* reckoned to be these four.

Phys. l.7. c. 3.

{ *Pulsio.*
Tractio.
Vectio.
Vertigo. }

Thrusting, Drawing, Carrying, Turning. Unto some of which all these artificial operations must necessarily be reduced, the strength of any power being equally appliable unto all of them; So that there is no work impossible to these contrivances, but there may be as much acted by this Art, as can be fancied by imagination.

CAP. XV.

Concerning the proportion of slowness and swiftness in Mechanical motions.

Having already discoursed concerning the *strength* of these Mechanical Faculties: It remains for the more perfect discovery of their natures, that we treat somewhat concerning those two differences of artificial motion:

Slow-

} Slowness, and Swiftness.

Without the right understanding of which, a man shall be exposed to many absurd mistakes, in attempting of those things which are either in themselves impossible, or else not to be performed with such means as are applyed unto them. I may safely affirm, that many, if not most mistakes in these Mechanical designs, do arise from a mis-apprehension of that difference which there will be betwixt the slowness or swiftness of the weight and power, in comparison to the proportion of their several strengths.

Hence it is, that so many engines invented for mines and water-works do so often fail in the performance of that for which they were intended, because the artificers many times do forget to allow so much time for the working of their engine, as may be proportionable to the difference betwixt the weight and power that
H 4 belong

belong unto them; whereas he that rightly understands the grounds of this Art, may as easily find out the difference of space and time, required to the motion of the weight and power, as he may their different strengths; and not only tell how any power may move any weight, but also in what a space of *time* it may move any space or *distance*.

If it were possible to contrive such an invention, whereby any conceivable weight may be moved by any conceivable power, both with the same quickness and speed (as it is in those things which are immediately stirred by the hand, without the help of any other instrument) the works of nature would be then too much subjected to the power of art: and men might be thereby incouraged (with the builders of *Babel*, or the rebel Gyants) to such bold designs as would not become a created being. And therefore the wisdom of Providence hath so confined these humane Arts, that what any invention hath

hath in the *strength* of its motion, is abated in the *slowness* of it; and what it hath in the extraordinary *quickness* of its motion, must be allowed for in the great *strength* that is required unto it.

For it is to be observed as a general rule, that the space of time or place, in which the weight is moved, in comparison to that in which the power doth move, is in the same proportion as they themselves are unto one another.

So that if there be any great difference betwixt the strength of the weight and the power, the same kind of difference will there be in the spaces of their motion.

To illustrate this by an example:

Let

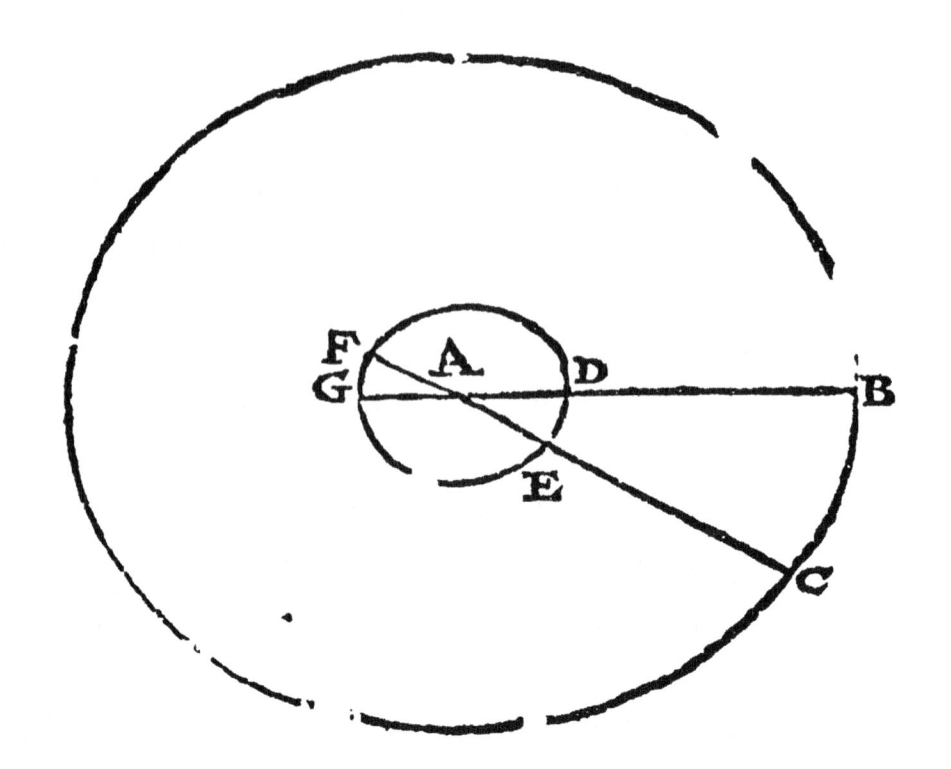

Let the line *G A B*, represent a ballance or leaver, the weight being supposed at the point *G*, the fulciment at *A*, and the power sustaining the weight at *B*. Suppose the point *G*, unto which the weight is fastned, to be elevated unto *F*, and the opposite point *B*, to be depressed unto *C*; 'tis evident that the arch *F G*, or (which is all one) *D E*, doth shew the space of the weight, and the arch *B C*, the motion of the power. Now both

Cap. 15. Mechanical Powers.

both these arches have the same proportion unto one other, as there is betwixt the weight and the power, or (which is all one) as there is betwixt their several distances from the fulciment. Suppose AG, unto AB, to be as one unto four, it may then be evident that FG, or DE, will be in the same proportion unto BC. For as any two Semidiameters are unto one another, so are the several circumferences described by them, as also any proportional parts of the same circumferences.

And as the weight and power do thus differ in the spaces of their motions, so likewise in the slowness of it; the one moving the whole distance BC, in the same time, wherein the other passes only GF. So that the motion of the power from B to C, is four times swifter than that of the weight from G to F. And thus will it be, if we suppose the disproportions to be far greater, whether or no we conceive it, either by a *continuation* of the same instrument and
fa-

faculty, as in the former example, or by a *multiplication* of divers, as in Pulleys, Wheels, &c. By how much the power is in it self less than the weight, by so much will the motion of the weight be slower than that of the power.

To this purpose I shall briefly touch at one of the Diagrams expressed before in the twelfth Chapter, concerning the multiplication of Leavers.

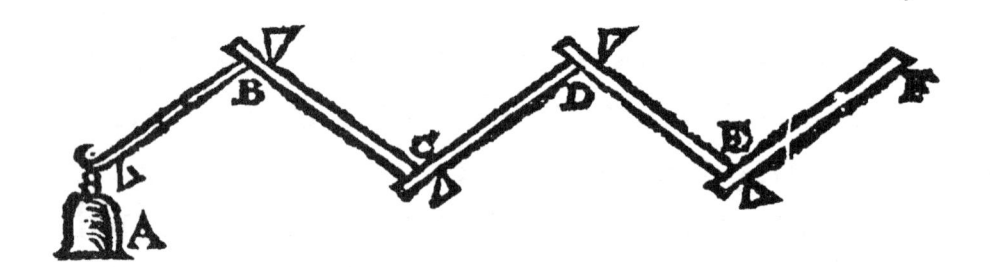

In which, as each instrument doth diminish the weight according to a decuple proportion, so also do they diminish the *space* and *slowness* of its motion. For if we should conceive the first Leaver B, to be depressed unto its lowest, suppose ten foot, yet the weight A, would not be raised

Cap. 15. *Mechanical Powers.*

sed above one foot; but now the second Leaver at its utmost could move but a tenth part of the first, and the third Leaver but a tenth part of the second, and so of the rest. So that the last Leaver *F*, being depressed, will pass a *space* 100000 greater, and by a motion, 100000 swifter than the weight at *A*.

Thus are we to conceive of all the other faculties, wherein there is constantly the same disproportion betwixt the weight and power, in respect of the spaces and slowness of their motions, as there is betwixt their several gravities. If the power be unto the weight but as one unto a hundred, then the space through which the weight moves, will be a hundred times less, and consequently the motion of the weight a hundred times slower than that of the power.

So that it is but a vain and impossible fancy for any one to think that he can move a great weight with a little power, in a little space; but in all these Mechanical attempts, that advantage

vantage which is gotten in the strength of the motion must be still allowed for in the slowness of it.

Though these contrivances do so extremely increase the power, yet they do proportionably protract the time. That which by such helps one man may do in a hundred days, may be done by the immediate strength of a hundred men in one day.

CAP. XVI.

That it is possible to contrive such an artificial motion, as shall be of a slowness proportionable to the swiftness of the heavens.

IT were a pretty subtilty to enquire after, whether or no it be not possible to contrive such an artificial motion, that should be in such a proportion slow, as the heavens are supposed to be swift.

For the exact resolution of which, it would be requisite that we should first pitch upon some *medium*, or indifferent

different motion, by the distance from which, we may judge of the proportions on either side, whether slowness or swiftness. Now because there is not any such *natural medium*, which may be absolutely styled an indifferent motion, but that the swiftness and slowness of every thing, is still proportioned either to the quantity of bodies, in which they are, or some other particular end for which they are designed; therefore we must take liberty to suppose such a motion, and this we may conceive to be about 1000 paces, or a mile in an hour.

The starry heaven, or 8*th* sphear, is thought to move 42398437 miles in the same space: So that if it may be demonstrated that it is possible to contrive such a motion, which going on in a constant direct course, shall pass but the 42398437 part of a mile in an hour, it will then be evident, that an artificial motion may be slow, in the same proportion as the heavens are swift.

Now

Now it was before manifested, that according to the difference betwixt the weight and the power, so will the difference be betwixt the slowness or swiftness of their motions; whence it will follow, that in such an engine, wherein the weight shall be 42398437 pounds, and the power that doth equiponderate it, but the 42398437 part of a pound (which is easie to contrive) in this engine the power being supposed to move with such a swiftness, as may be answerable to a mile an hour, the weight will pass but the 42398437 part of a mile in the same space, and so consequently will be proportionably slow unto the swiftness of the Heavens.

Preface to Euclid. It is related by our Country-man J. Dee, that he and *Cardan* being both together in their travels, they did see an instrument which was at first sold for 20 talents of gold, wherein there was one wheel, which constantly moving round amongst the rest, did not finish one revolution under the space of seven thousand years.

But

Cap. 16. Mechanical Powers.

But if we farther confider fuch an inftrument of wheels as was mentioned before in the 14 Chapter, with which the whole world might be eafily moved, we fhall then find that the motion of the weight by that, muft be much more flow, than the heavens are fwift. For though we fuppofe (faith *Stevinus*) the handle of fuch an engine with 12 wheels to be turned about 4000 times in an hour, (which is as often as a mans pulfe doth beat) yet in ten years fpace the weight by this would not be moved above $\frac{10512}{2400}$ 00000000000000000 parts of one foot, which is nothing near fo much as an hairs breadth. And it could not pafs an inch in 1000000 years, faith *Merfennus*.

De ftat: praft.

Phænom. Mechan. prop. 11.

The truth of which we may more eafily conceive, if we confider the frame and manner of this 12 wheel'd engine. Suppofe that in each axis or nut, there were ten teeth, and on each wheel a thoufand: then the fails of this engine muft be turned a hundred times, before the firft wheel (reckoning

ing downward) could be moved round once, and ten thousand times before the second wheel can finish one revolution, and so through the 12 wheels, according to this multiplied proportion.

So that besides the wonder which there is in the force of these Mechanical motions, the extreme slowness of them is no less admirable; If a man consider that a body would remain in such a constant direct motion, that there could not be one minute of time wherein it did not rid some space, and pass on further, and yet that this body in many years together should not move so far as an hairs breadth.

Which notwithstanding may evidently appear from the former instance. For since it is a natural principle, that there can be no penetration of bodies; and since it is supposed, that each of the parts in this engine do touch one another in their superficies, therefore it must necessarily follow, that the weight does begin and

Cap. 16. *Mechanical Powers.*

and continue to move with the power; and (however it is insensible) yet it is certain there must be such a motion so extremely slow, as is here specified. So full is this art of rare and incredible subtilties.

I know it is the assertion of *Cardan, Motus valde tardi, necessario quietes habent intermedias.* Extreme slow motions have necessarily some intermediate stops and rests: But this is only said, not proved; and he speaks it from sensible experiments, which in this case are fallible. Our senses being very incompetent judges of the several proportions, whether greatness or littleness, slowness or swiftness, which there may be amongst things in nature. For ought we know, there may be some *Organical* bodies, as much less than ours, as the earth is bigger. We see what strange discoveries of extreme minute bodies, (as lice, wheel-worms, mites, and the like) are made by the *Microscope*, wherein their several parts (which are altogether invisible to the

De varietate rerum l. 9. c. 47.

bare

bare eye) will distinctly appear: and perhaps there may be other insects that live upon them as they do upon us. 'Tis certain that our senses are extremely disproportioned for comprehending the whole compass and latitude of things. And because there may be such difference in the *motion* as well as in the *magnitude* of bodies; therefore though such extreme slowness may seem altogether impossible to sense and common apprehension, yet this can be no sufficient argument against the reality of it.

CAP. XVII.

Of swiftness, how it may be increased to any kind of proportion. Concerning the great force of Archimedes *his Engines. Of the Ballista.*

BY that which hath been already explained concerning the slowness of motion, we may the better understand the nature of swiftness, both of them (as is the nature of opposites)

Cap. 17. *Mechanical Powers.*

sites) being produced by contrary causes. As the greatness of the weight in respect of the power, and the great distance of the power from the fulciment, in comparison to that of the weight, does cause a slow motion: So the greatness of the power above the weight, and the greater distance of the weight from the center, in comparison to that of the power, does cause a swift motion. And as it is possible to contrive a motion unto any kind of slowness, by finding out an answerable disproportion betwixt the weight and power: so likewise unto any kind of swiftness. For so much as the weight does exceed the power, by so much will the motion of the weight be slower; and so much as the power does exceed the weight, by so much will the motion of the weight be swifter.

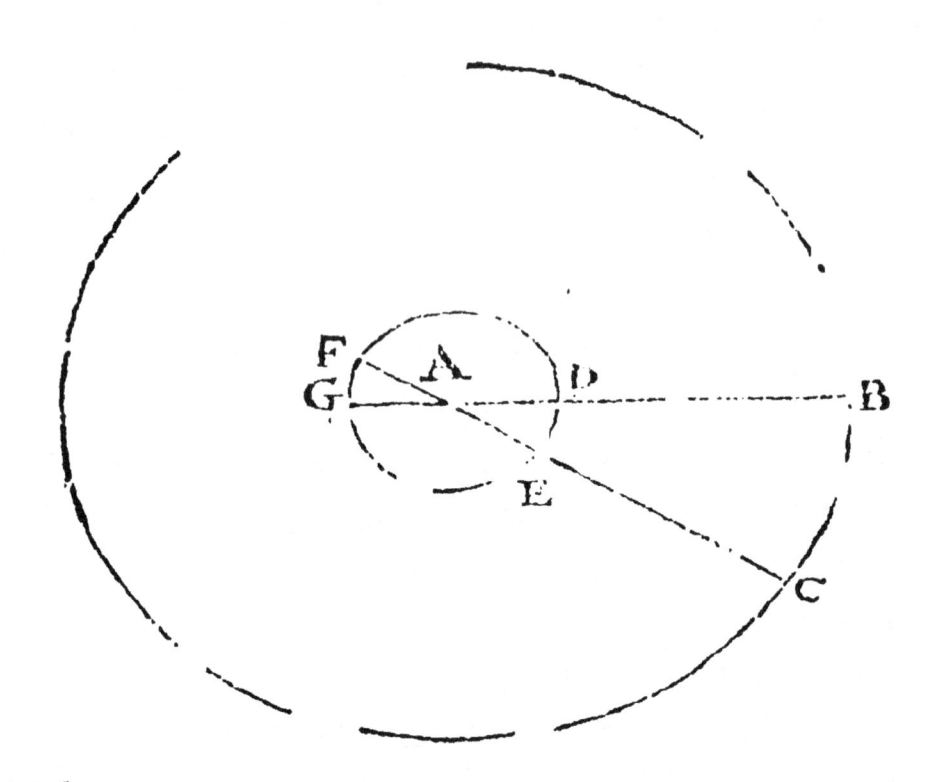

In the Diagram set down before, if we suppose *F* to be the place of the power, and *C* of the weight, the point *A* being the fulciment or center, then in the same space of time, wherein the power does move from *F* to *G*, the weight will pass from *C* to *B*. These distances having the same disproportion unto one another, as there is betwixt *AF*, and *AC*, which is supposed to be quadruple. So that in this example, the weight will move

four

Cap. 17. *Mechanical Powers.*

four times swifter than the power. And according as the power does exceed the weight in any greater disproportion, so will the swiftness of the weight be augmented.

Hence may we conceive the reason of that great force which there is in Slings, which have so much a greater swiftness, than a stone thrown from the hand, by how much the end of the Sling is farther off from the shoulder-joynt, which is the center of motion. The Sacred history concerning *David*'s victory over *Goliah*, may sufficiently evidence the force of these. *Vegetius* relates that it was usual this way to strike a man dead, and beat the soul out of his body, without so much as breaking his armour, or fetching blood. *Membris integris lethale tamen vulnus important, & sine invidia sanguinis, hostis lapidis ictu intereat.* [1 Sam. 17. 49. Lipsius Polior. l. 4. Dialog. 2.]

In the use of these, many of the Ancients have been of very exquisite and admirable skill. We read of *seven hundred Benjamites left-handed, that could* [Judges 20. 16.]

sling a stone at a hairs breadth, *and not miss*. And there is the like storied of a whole Nation among the *Indians*, who from their excellency in this art were stiled *Baleares*. They were so strict in teaching this art unto their young ones, *Ut cibum puer à matre non accipit, nisi quem ipsâ monstrante percussit*, That the Mother would not give any meat to her child, till (being set at some distance) he could hit it with flinging.

For the farther illustration of this subject, concerning the *swiftness* of motion, I shall briefly specifie some particulars concerning the engines of War used by the Ancients. Amongst these, the most famous and admirable were those invented by *Archimedes*, by which he did perform such strange exploits, as (were they not related by so many, and such judicious Authors) would scarce seem credible even to these more learned ages. The acts of that famous Engineer, are largely set down by [a] *Polybius*, [b] *Tzetzes*, [c] *Proclus*, [d] *Plutarch*, [e] *Livy*,

Cap. 17. *Mechanical Powers.*

vy, and divers others. From the first of whom alone, we may have sufficient evidence for the truth of those relations. For besides that he is an Author noted to be very grave and serious in his discourse; and does solemnly promise in one place that he will relate nothing but what either he himself was an eye-witness of, or else what he had received from those that were so; I say, besides all this, it is considerable, that he himself was born not above thirty years after the siege of *Syracuse*. And afterwards having occasion to tarry some weeks in that City, when he travelled with *Scipio*, he might there perhaps see those engines himself, or at least take his Information from such as were eye-witnesses of their force: So that there can be no colourable pretence for any one to distrust the particulars related of them.

In brief, the sum of their reports is this: When the *Roman* forces under the conduct of *Marcellus*, had laid siege unto that famous City, (of which

Histor.l.4 juxta initium.

which both by their former successes, and their present strength, they could not chuse but promise themselves a speedy victory); yet the arts of this one Mathematician, notwithstanding all their policies and resolutions, did still beat them back to their great disadvantage. Whether they were near the wall, or farther from it, they were still exposed to the force of his engines, *κὴ μακρὰν ἀφεςῶτας, κὴ ἐγγὺς ὄντας, ἒ μόνον ἀπράκτες παρεσκύαζε πρὸς τὰς ἰδίας ἐπιβολὰς, ἀλλὰ κὴ διέρθειρε τὲς πλείςες αὐτῶν.* From the multitude of those stones and arrows, which he shot against them, was he styled *ἑκατόνχειρ*, or *Briareus*. Those defensive engines that were made by the *Romans* in the form of Penthouses for to cover the assailants from the weapons of the besieged, these would he presently batter in pieces with great stones and blocks. Those high-towers erected in some of the ships, out of which the *Romans* might more conveniently fight with the defendants on the wall, these also were

Cæl. Rhod. Ant. lect. l. 2. c. 16. Pluteus. Testudo.

Cap. 17. *Mechanical Powers.*

so broken by his engines, that no Cannon or other instrument of Gunpowder, (saith a learned man) had they been then in use, could have done greater mischief. *Sir Walt. Raleigh histor. l.5. c 3. sect. 16.* In brief, he did so molest them with his frequent and prodigious batteries, that the common soldiers were utterly discouraged from any hopes of success.

What was the particular frame and manner of these engines, cannot certainly be determined; but to contrive such as may perform the like strange effects, were not very difficult to any one who is throughly versed in the grounds of this art. Though perhaps those of *Archimedes* in respect of divers circumstances, were much more exact and proper for the purposes to which they were intended, than the invention of others could be; He himself being so extraordinarily subtil and ingenious above the common sort of men.

'Tis probable that the general kind of these engines, were the same with those that were used afterwards

wards amongst the *Romans* and other Nations. These were commonly divided into two sorts: styled.

{ *Ballistæ.*
{ *Catapultæ.*

Both which names are sometimes used promiscuously; but according to their propriety † *Ballista* does signifie an engine for the shooting of stones, and *Catapulta* for darts or arrows.

The former of these was fitted either to carry divers lesser stones, or else one greatest one. Some of these engines made for great stones, have been proportioned to so vast and immense a weight, as may seem almost incredible: which occasioned that in *Lucan.*

Vid. Naudæum de Stud. Militar. l. 2 ἀπὸ τῶ βάλλειν called also λιθόβολος πετροβόλ῀. Fundibalus. Petraria.

lib. 3.

At saxum quoties ingenti verberis ictu
Excutitur, qualis rupes quam vertico montis
Abscidit impulsu ventorum adjuta vetustas,
Frangit cuncta ruens; nec tantum corpora pressa
Examinat, totos cum sanguine dissipat artus.

With these, they could easily batter down the Walls and Towers of any Fort. So *Ovid.*

Quam

Cap. 17. Mechanical Powers. 125

Quam grave balliſtæ mœnia pulſat onus.

And *Statius*—— *Quo turbine bellica quondam,*
Librati ſaliunt portarum in clauſtra molares.

The ſtones that were caſt from theſe, were of any form, *Enormes & ſepulchrales*, Milſtones or Tomb-ſtones. Sometimes for the farther annoyance and terror of any beſieged place, they would by theſe throw into it dead bodies, either of men or horſes, and ſometimes only parts of them, as mens heads.

Athenæus mentions one of theſe *Balliſtæ* that was proportioned unto a ſtone of three talents weight, each talent being 120 pounds (ſaith *Vitruvius*) ſo that the whole will amount to 360 pounds. But it is ſtoried of *Archimedes*, that he caſt a ſtone into one of *Marcellus* his ſhips, which was found to weigh ten talents. There is ſome difference amongſt * Authors, concerning what kind of talent this ſhould be underſtood, but it is certain that

LipſiusPoliorcet.l.3. Dial. 3.

Deipnoſoph.l. 5.

Archit.l. 10. c. ult.
λίθον δικατάλαντον.
Plut. Marcell.
* Dav. Rivaltus Comen in Archim Oper Ext.

that in *Plutarchs* time, (from whom we have this relation) one talent did amount to 120 pounds (saith *Suidas*) according to which account, the stone it self was of no less than twelve hundred pound weight. A weapon (one would think) big enough for those rebel Gyants that fought against the gods. Now the greatest Cannon in use, does not carry above 64 pound weight, which is far short of the strength in these Mathematical contrivances. Amongst the Turks indeed, there have been sometimes used such powder-instruments, as may equal the force of those invented by *Archimedes*. Gab. *Naudæus* tells us of one bullet shot from them at the siege of *Constantinople*, which was of above 1200 pound weight; This he affirms from the relation of an Archbishop, who was then present, and did see it; the piece could not be drawn by less than an hundred and fifty yoak of oxen, which might almost have served to draw away the Town it self. But though there hath been perhaps some

Naudæus de studio Milit. l. 2.

De Stud. Mil. l. 2.

Cap. 17. *Mechanical Powers.* 127

one or two Cannons of such a prodigious magnitude, yet it is certain that the biggest in common use, does come far short of that strength, which was ordinarily in these Mechanical engines.

There are divers figures of these *Ballistæ*, set out by *Vigetius*, *Lipsius*, and others; but being without any explication, it is not very facil to discover in what their forces did consist.

See Rob. Valteurius de re Milit. l. 10 c. 4.

I have here expressed one of them most easie to be apprehended; from the understanding of which, you may the better guess at the nature of the rest.

That

128 *Archimedes; or,* Lib. I.

That great box or cavity at *A*, is supposed to be full of some heavy weight, and is forced up by the turning

ning of the axis and spokes B C. The stone or bullet to be discharged being in a kind of sling at *D*, which when the greater weight *A*, descends, will be violently whirled upwards, till that end of the sling at *E*, coming to the top, will fly off, and discharge the stone as the skilful Artist should direct it.

C A P. XVIII.
Concerning the Catapultæ, or Engines for Arrows.

THE other kind of engine was called *Catapultæ*, ἀπὸ τ πέλτης, which signifies a spear or dart, because it was used for the shooting of such weapons: some of these were proportioned unto spears of twelve cubits long; they did carry with so great a force, *ut interdum nimio ardore scintillant,* (saith *Ammianus*) that the weapons discharged from them were sometimes (if you can believe it) set on fire by the swiftness of their motion.

In Greek ακτυπέλτης.
Athenæus Deipnos. l. 5.

Lib. 230.

Lipsius Poliorcet. *l.* 3. Dial. 2.

K   The

The first invention of these is commonly ascribed to *Dionysius* the younger, who is said to have made them amongst his other preparations against *Carthage*. But we have good reason to think them of more ancient use, because we read in Scripture, that *Uzziah made in Jerusalem, engines invented by cunning men, to shoot arrows and great stones withal*; tho it is likely these inventions were much bettered by the experience of afterages.

The usual form of these *Catapultæ*, was much after the manner of great Bows placed on Carriages, and wound up by the strength of several persons. And from that great force which we find in lesser Bows, we may easily ghess at the greater power of these other engines. 'Tis related of the Turkish Bow, that it can strike an arrow through a piece of steel or brass two inches thick; and being headed only with wood, it pierces Timber of eight inches. Which though it may seem incredible,

Diod. Sic. Biblioth. l. 14. Sardus de Invert Rerum l. 2.

2 Chron. 26. 15.

Sir Franc. Bacon's Nat. Hist. Exp. 704.

ble, yet it is attested by the experience of divers unquestionable witnesses. *Barclay* in his *Icon animorum*, a man of sufficient credit, affirms, that he was an eye-witness, how one of these Bows with a little arrow did pierce through a piece of steel three fingers thick. And yet these Bows being somewhat like the long Bows in use amongst us, were bent only by a mans immediate strength, without the help of any bender or rack that are used to others.

Some *Turkish* Bows are of that strength, as to pierce a plank of six inches in thickness, (I speak what I have seen) saith *M. Jo. Greaves* in his *Pyromodographia*. How much greater force then may we conceive to be impressed by the *Catapultæ*?

These were sometimes framed for the discharging of two or three arrows together, so that each of them might be directed unto a several aim. But it were as easie to contrive them after the like manner for the carriage of twenty arrows, or more, as in this figure.

132   *Archimedes; or,*   Lib. I.

* Who was before stil'd Potorcetes This kind of Turret was first used at the siege of Cyprus, and is thus described by Diodorus. Sicul. Biblioth. l. 20.

Both these kinds of engines when they were used at the siege of any City, were commonly carried in a great wooden Turret (first invented by * *Demetrius*). It was driven upon four wheels at the bottom, each of its sides being forty five cubits, its height ninety. The whole was divided into nine several partitions, every one of which did contain divers engines for battery: from its use in the battering and taking of Cities it is
stiled

Cap. 18. *Mechanical Powers.*

ſtiled by the name of *Helepolis*.

He that would be informed in the nature of Bows, let him conſult *Merſennus de Balliſtica & Acontiſmologia*, where there are divers ſubtil inquiries and demonſtrations, concerning the ſtrength required to the bending of them to any diſtance; the force they have in the diſcharge, according to ſeveral bents, the ſtrength required to be in the ſtring of them, the ſeveral proportions of ſwiftneſs and diſtance in an arrow ſhot vertically, or horizontally, or tranſverſally.

Thoſe ſtrange effects of the *Turkiſh* Bow (mentioned before) ſo much exceeding the force of others, which yet require far greater ſtrength for the bending of them, may probably be aſcribed either to the natural cauſe of *attraction by ſimilitude of ſubſtance* (as the Lord *Bacon* conjectures); For in theſe experiments the head of the arrow ſhould be of the ſame ſubſtance (whether ſteel or wood) with that which it pierces: Or elſe to that *juſt proportion* betwixt the

K 3   weight

weight of the arrow, and the strength of the bow, which must needs much conduce to the force of it, and may perhaps be more exactly discovered in these, than it is commonly in others.

CAP. XIX.

A comparison betwixt these ancient Engines, and the Gun-powder instruments now in use.

IT shall not be altogether impertinent to inquire somewhat concerning the advantages and disadvantages betwixt those Military offensive engines, used amongst the Ancients, and those of these later ages.

In which inquiry there are two particulars to be chiefly examined:

1. The force of these several contrivances, or the utmost that may be done by them.

2. Their price, or the greatness of the charges required unto them.

1. As for the force of these ancient

Cap. 19. Mechanical Powers.

ent inventions, it may sufficiently appear from those many credible relations mentioned before; to which may be added that in *Josephus*, which he sets down from his own eye-sight, being himself a chief Captain at the siege of *Jotapata*, where these events happened. He tells us, that besides the multitude of persons, who were slain by these *Roman* Engines, being not able to avoid their force, by reason they were placed so far off, and out of sight; besides this, they did also carry such great stones, with so great a violence, that they did therewith batter down their Walls and Towers. A great bellied woman walking about the City in the day-time, had her child struck out of her womb, and carried half a furlong from her. A soldier standing by his Captain *Josephus*, on the wall, had his head struck off by another stone sent from these *Roman* Engines, and his brains carried three furlongs off.

De Bello Judaico, l. 3. c. 9.

To this purpose *Cardan* relates out of *Ammianus Marcellinus*, Tanto impetu

De var. l. 12. c. 58.

impetu fertur lapis ut uno viso lapide quamvis intacti barbari fuerint ab eo, destiterunt à pugna & abierunt. Many foreign people being so amazed at the strange force of these Engines, that they durst not contest with those who were masters of such inventions. 'Tis frequently asserted, that bullets have been melted in the air, by that extremity of violent motion imprest from these slings.

Fundáque contorto transverberat aëra plumbo,
Et mediis liquidæ glandes in nubibus errant.

So *Lucan*, speaking of the same Engines.

Inde faces & saxa volant, spatioque solutæ.
Aëris & calidæ liquefactæ pondere glandes.

Which relations, though they may seem somewhat poetical and improbable, yet *Aristotle* himself (*De Cælo, lib.* 2. *c.* 7) doth suppose them as unquestionable. From whence it may be inferred, that the force of these Engines

Cap. 19. *Mechanical Powers.*

gines does rather exceed than come short of our Gunpowder inventions.

Add to this that opinion of a learned man (which I cited before) that *Archimedes* in the siege of *Syracuse*, did more mischief with his Engines, than could have been wrought by any Cannons, had they been then in use.

Sir Walt. Raleigh's Hist. l. 5. c. 3. Sect. 16. *See* Lipsius de militiâ Romana l. 5.

In this perhaps there may be some disadvantage, because these Mathematical Engines cannot be so easily and speedily wound up, and so certainly levelled as the other may.

2. As for the price or charges of both these, it may be considered under three particulars:
1. Their making.
2. Their carriage or conveyance.
3. Their charge and discharging.

In all which respects, the Cannons now in use, are of much greater cost than these other inventions.

1. The making or price of these Gunpowder instruments is extremely expensive, as may be easily judged by the weight of their materials. A whole Cannon

Cannon weighing commonly 8000 *l.* a half Cannon 5000, a Culverin 4500, a Demiculverin 3000; which whether it be in iron or brass, must needs be very costly, only for the matter of them; besides the farther charges required for the form and making of them, which in the whole must needs amount to several hundred pounds. Whereas these Mathematical inventions consisting chiefly of Timber, and Cords, may be much more cheaply made; The several degrees of them which shall answer in proportion to the strength of those other, being at the least ten times cheaper; that is, ten Engines that shall be of equal force either to a Cannon or Demicannon, Culverin or Demiculverin, may be framed at the same price that one of these will amount to: So that in this respect there is a great inequality.

2. As for the Carriage or conveyance; a whole Cannon does require at the least 90 men, or 16 horses, for the draught of it; a half Cannon 56 men,

Cap. 19. Mechanical Powers. 139

men, or 9 horses; a Culverin 50 men, or 8 horses; a Demiculverin 36 men, or 7 horses; Supposing the way to be hard and plain, in which notwithstanding the motion will be very slow. But if the passage prove rising and steep, or rotten and dirty, then they will require a much greater strength and charge for the conveyance of them. Whereas these other inventions are in themselves more light (if there be occasion for the draught of them) being easily taken asunder into several parts. And besides their materials are to be found every where, so that they need not be carried up and down at all, but may be easily made in the place where they are to be used.

3. The materials required to the charging of these Gun-powder instruments are very costly. A whole Cannon requiring for every charge 40 pounds of powder, and a bullet of 64 pounds; a half Cannon 18 pounds of powder, and a bullet of 24 pounds; a Culverin 16 pounds of powder, and

a bullet

a bullet of 19 pounds; a Demiculverin 9 pounds of powder, and a bullet of 12 pounds: whereas thofe other Engines may be charged only with ſtones, or (which may ſerve for terrour) with dead bodies, or any ſuch materials as every place will afford without any coſt.

So then, put all theſe together: If it be ſo that theſe ancient inventions did not come ſhort of theſe other in regard of force, and if they do ſo much excel them in divers others reſpects; It ſhould ſeem then, that they are much more commodious than theſe latter inventions, and ſhould be preferred before them. But this enquiry cannot be fully determined without particular experience of both.

CAP.

CAP. XX.

That it is possible to contrive such an artificial motion, as may be equally swift with the supposed motion of the heavens.

FOR the conclusion of this Discourse, I shall briefly examine (as before concerning slowness) whether it be possible to contrive such an artificial motion, as may be equal unto the supposed swiftness of the heavens. This question hath been formerly proposed and answered by *Cardan*, where he applies it unto the swiftness of the Moons Orb; but that Orb being the lowest of all, and consequently of a dull and sluggish motion in comparison to the rest; therefore it will perhaps be more convenient to understand the question concerning the eighth sphere or starry heaven.

For the true resolution of this, it would be first observed, that a material substance is altogether incapable

De variet. Rerum l. 9. c. 47.

The earth a Planet, prop. 9.

ble of so great a celerity, as is usually ascribed to the Cœlestial Orbs, (as I have proved elsewhere.) And therefore the quæry is not to be understood for any real and experimental, but only notional and Geometrical contrivance.

Now that the swiftness of motion may be thus increased, according to any conceivable proportion, will be manifest from what hath been formerly delivered concerning the grounds and nature of slowness and swiftness. For according as we shall suppose the power to exceed the weight; so may the motion of the weight be swifter than that of the power.

But to answer more particularly: Let us imagine every wheel in this following figure to have an hundred teeth in it, and every nut ten:

Cap. 20. Mechanical Powers. 143

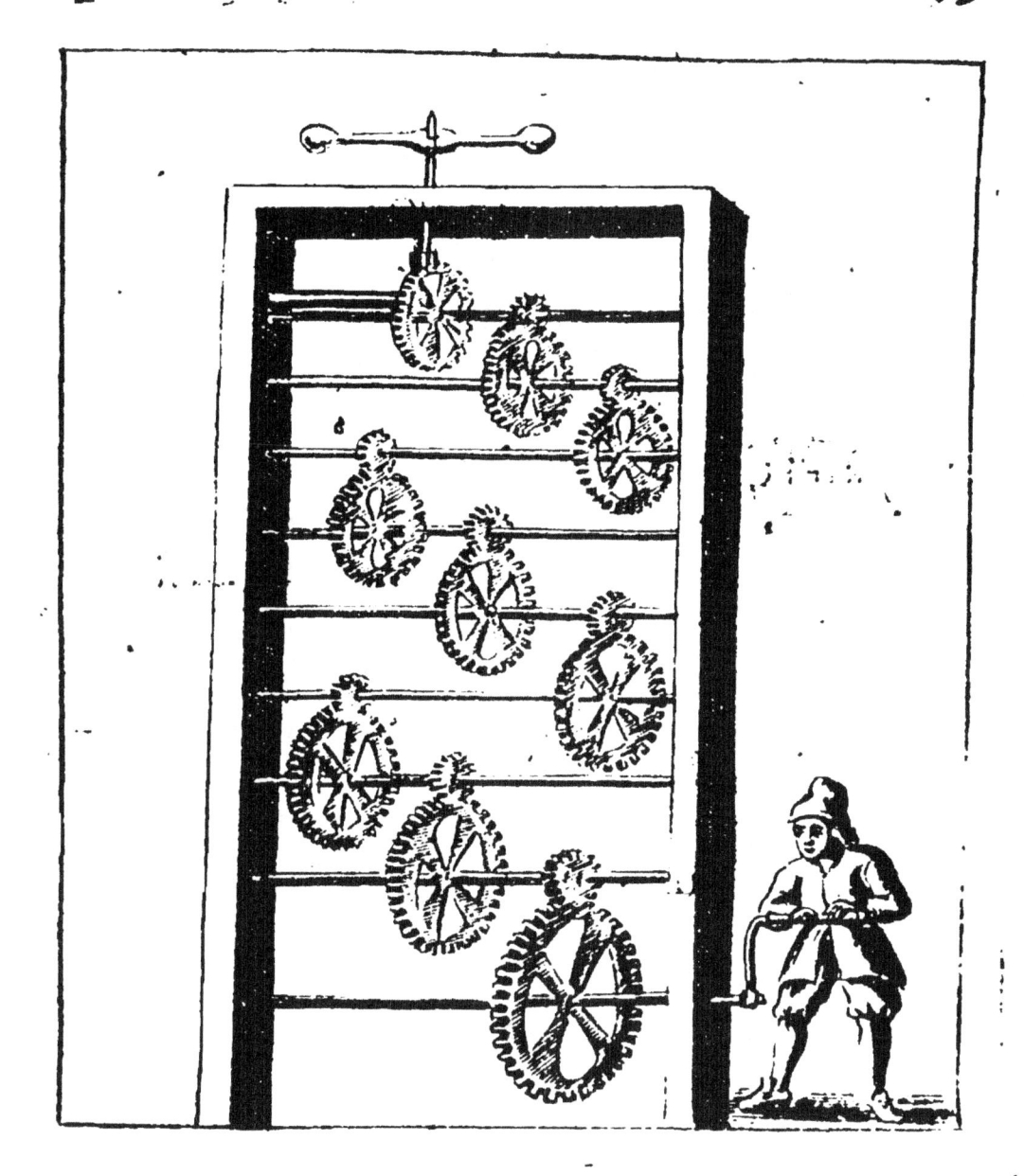

It may then be evident, that one revolution of the first wheel, will turn the nut, and consequently the second wheel on the same axis ten times, the third

third wheel a hundred times, the fourth 1000 times, the fifth 10000, the sixth a hundred thousand times, the seventh 1000000 times, the eighth 10000000 times, the 9th 100000000 times, the Sails 1000000000 times; So that if we suppose the compass of these Sails to be five foot, or one pace; and that the first wheel is turned about after the rate of one thousand times in an hour: It will then be evident, that the sails shall be turned 1000000000000 times, and consequently shall pass 1000000000 miles in the same space. Whereas a star in the Æquator (according to common *Hypothesis*) does move but 42398437 miles in an hour; and therefore it is evident that 'tis possible Geometrically to contrive such an artificial motion, as shall be of greater swiftness than the supposed revolutions of the heavens.

DÆDA-

DÆDALUS.
OR, Mechanical Motions.

The Second Book.

CHAP. I.

The divers kind of Automata, *or Self-movers. Of Mills, and the contrivance of several motions by rarified air. A brief digression concerning wind-guns.*

Amongst the variety of artificial motions, those are of most use and pleasure, in which, by the application of some continued strength, there is bestowed a regular and lasting motion.

These we call the αὐτόματα, or *self-movers*: which name in its utmost latitude, is sometimes ascribed unto those motions that are contrived from the strength of living creatures, as Chariots, Carts, &c. But in its strictness and propriety, it is only appliable unto such inventions, wherein the motion is caused either by something

L that

that belongs unto its own frame, or else by some external inanimate agent.

Whence these ἀυτόματα are easily distinguishable into two sorts.

1. Those that are moved by something which is extrinsecal unto their own frame, as Mills by water or wind.

2. Those that receive their motion from something that does belong to the frame it self, as Clocks, Watches, by weights, springs, or the like.

Of both which sorts there have been many excellent inventions: In the recital of them, I shall insist chiefly on such as are most eminent for their rarity and subtilty.

Amongst the ἀυτόματα that receive their motion from some external agent, those of more common use are Mills.

And first, the Water-mills, which are thought to be before the other, though neither the first Author, nor so much as the time wherein they were invented is fully known. And therefore *Polydor Virgil* refers them amongst other fatherless inventions. *Pliny* indeed doth mention them; as being commonly used in his time, and yet others

De invent. Rerum, l. 3. c. 18. Nat. Hist. l. 18. c. 10.

others affirm that *Bellisarius* in the reign of *Justinian*, did first invent them: whence *Pancirollus* concludes, that it is likely their use was for some space intermitted, and being afterwards renewed again, they were then thought to be first discovered.

De repert.
Tit. 22

However 'tis certain, that this invention hath much abridged and advantaged the labours of men, who were before condemned unto this slavery, as now unto the Galleys. And as the force of waters hath been useful for this, so likewise may it be contrived to divers other purposes. Herein doth the skill of an artificer chiefly consist, in the application of these common motions unto various and beneficial ends, making them serviceable not only for the grinding of corn, but for the preparing of iron or other oar, the making of paper, the elevating of water, or the like.

Ad Pistrinum

To this purpose also are the Mills that are driven by wind, which are so much more convenient than the other, by how much their situations may be more easie and common. The motions of these may likewise be accommodated to as various uses as the other, there being scarce any labour, to the performance of which an ingenious artificer cannot apply them. To the sawing of Timber, the plowing of land, or any other the like service, which cannot be dispatched the ordinary way, without much toil and tediousness. And it is a wonderful thing to consider, how much mens labours might be eased and contracted in sundry particulars, if such as were well skilled in the principles and practices of these Mechanical experiments, would but throughly apply their studies unto the enlargement of such inventions.

There are some other motions by wind or air, which (though they are not so common as the other), yet may prove of excellent curiosity, and singular use. Such was that musical instrument invented by *Cornelius Drebble*, which being set in the sun-shine, would of it self render a soft and pleasant

Maercel. Vrankhem Epist. ad Joh. Ernestum.

Cap. 1. *Mechanical Motions.*

pleasant harmony, but being removed into the shade would presently become silent. The reason of it was this, the warmth of the sun, working upon some moisture within it, and rarifying the inward air unto so great an extension, that it must needs seek for a vent or issue, did thereby give several motions unto the instrument.

Somewhat of this nature are the *Eolipiles*, which are concave Vessels, consisting of some such material as may endure the fire, having a small hole, at which they are filled with water, and out of which (when the Vessels are heated) the air doth issue forth with a strong and lasting violence. These are frequently used for the exciting and contracting of heat in the melting of glasses or metals. They may also be contrived to be serviceable for sundry other pleasant uses, as for the moving of sails in a chimney corner, the motion of which sails may be applied to the turning of a spit, or the like.

But there is a better invention to this

Like that statue of Memnon, in Egypt, which makes a strange noise whenever the sun begins to shine upon it. Tacit. Annal. 2. Strabo affirms that he had both seen and heard it.

this purpose mentioned in *Cardan*, whereby a spit may be turned (without the help of weights) by the motion of the air that ascends the Chimney; and it may be useful for the roasting of many or great joynts: for as the fire must be increased according to the quantity of meat, so the force of the instrument will be augmented proportionably to the fire. In which contrivance there are these conveniences above the Jacks of ordinary use.

1. It makes little or no noise in the motion.

2. It needs no winding up, but will constantly move of it self, while there is any fire to rarifie the air.

3. It is much cheaper than the other instruments that are commonly used to this purpose. There being required unto it only a pair of sails, which must be placed in that part of the Chimney where it begins to be straightned, and one wheel, to the axis of which the spit line must be fastned, according to this following Diagram.

De Variet. Rerum, l. 12. c. 58.

The

The motion of these sails may likewise be serviceable for sundry other purposes, besides the turning of a spit, for the chiming of bells or other musical devices; and there cannot be any more pleasant contrivance for continual and cheap musick. It may be useful also for the reeling of yarn, the rocking of a cradle, with divers the like domestick occasions. For (as was said before) any constant motion being given, it is easie for an ingenious artificer to apply it unto various services.

These sails will always move both day and night, if there is but any fire under them, and sometimes though there be none. For if the air without, be much colder than that within the room, then must this which is more warm and rarified, naturally ascend through the chimney, to give place unto the more condensed and heavy, which does usually blow in at every chink or cranny, as experience shews.

Unto this kind of motion may be reduced all those representations of living creatures, whether birds, or beasts, invented by *Ctesibius*, which were for the most part performed by the motion of air, being forced up either by *rarefaction*, with fire, or else by *compression*, through the fall of of some heavier body, as water, which by possessing the place of the air, did thereby drive it to seek for some other vent.

I cannot here omit (though it be not altogether so pertinent) to mention that late ingenious invention of the wind-gun, which is charged by the forcible compression of air, being injected through a Syringe; the strife and distention of the imprisoned air serving by the help of little falls or shuts within, to stop and keep close the vents by which it was admitted. The force of it in the discharge is almost equal to our powder-guns. I have found upon frequent trials (saith *Mersennus*) that a leaden bullet shot from one of these Guns against a stone wall, the space of 24 paces from it, will be beaten into a thin plate. It would be a considerable addition to this experiment which the same Author mentions a little after, whereby he will make the same charge of air to serve for the discharge of several arrows or bullets after one another,

Phænomena pneumatica, prop. 32.

nother, by giving the air only so much room, as may immediately serve to impress a violence in sending away the arrow or bullet, and then screwing it down again to its former confinement, to fit it for another shooting. But against this there may be many considerable doubts, which I cannot stand to discuss.

CAP. II.

Of a sailing Chariot, that may without horses be driven on the land by the wind, as ships are on the sea.

THE force of wind in the motion of sails may be applied also to the driving of a Chariot, by which a man may sail on the land as well as by a ship on the water. The labour of horses or other beasts, which are usually applied to this purpose, being artificially supplied by the strength of winds.

That such Chariots are commonly used in the Champain plains of *China* is frequently affirmed by divers credible Authors. *Boterus* mentions, that they have been tried also in *Spain*, though

De incremento Urbium, l. 1. c. 0.

Cap. 2. Mechanical Motions.

though with what success he doth not specifie. But above all other experiments to this purpose that sailing Chariot at *Sceveling* in *Holland*, is more eminently remarkable. It was made by the direction of *Stephinus*, and is celebrated by many Authors. *Walchius* affirms it to be of so great a swiftness for its motion, and yet of so great a capacity for its burden. *Ut in medio freto secundis ventis commissas naves, velocitate multis parasangis post se relinquat, & paucarum horarum spatio, viginti aut triginta milliaria Germanica continuo cursu emetiatur, concreditosq; sibi plus minus vectores sex aut decem, in petitum locum transferat, facillimo illius ad clavum qui sedet nutu, quaquaversum minimo labore velis commissum, mirabile hoc continenti currus navigium dirigentis.* That it did far exceed the speed of any ship, though we should suppose it to be carried in the open sea with never so prosperous wind: and that in some few hours space it would convey 6 or 10 persons 20 or 30 German miles, and all this with very little labour of him that sitteth at the Stern,

Fabularum decas, Fab. 9.

Stern, who may easily guide the course of it as he pleaseth.

That eminent inquisitive man *Peireskius*, having travelled to *Sceveling* for the sight and experience of this Chariot, would frequently after with much wonder mention the extreme swiftness of its motion. *Commemorare solebat stuporem quo correptus fuerat cum vento translatus citatissimo non persentiscere tamen, nempe tam citus erat quam ventus.* Though the wind were in it self more swift and strong, yet to passengers in this Chariot it would not be at all discernable, because they did go with an equal swiftness to the wind it self. Men that ran before it, seeming to go backwards; things which seem at a great distance being presently overtaken and left behind. In two hours space it would pass from *Sceveling* to *Putten*, which are distant from one another above 14 *Horaria milliaria* (saith the same Author) that is, more than two and forty miles.

Grotius is very copious and elegant in the celebrating of this invention, and the

Pet. Gassendus. Vita Peireskii, l. 2.

Cap. 2. Mechanical Motions.

the Author of it, in divers Epigrams.

> *Ventivolam Typhis deduxit in æquora navim,*
> *Jupiter in stellas, æthereamque domum*
> *In terrestre solum virtus Stevinia, nam nec*
> *Tiphy tuum fuerat, nec Jovis istud opus.*

Grotii Poemata. Ep. 19.

And in another place,

> *Imposuit plaustro vectantem carbasa, malum*
> *An potius navi, subdidit ille rotas?*
> ——— *Scandit aques navis currus ruit aere prono,*
> *Et merito dicas hic volat, illa natat.*

Ep. 5.

These relations did at the first seem unto me (and perhaps they will so to others) somewhat strange & incredible. But upon farther enquiry I have heard them frequently attested from the particular eyesight and experience of such eminent persons, whose names I dare not cite in a business of this nature, which in those parts is so very common, and little observed.

I have not met with any Author who doth treat particularly concerning the manner of framing this Chariot, though *Grotius* mentions an elegant description of it in copper by one *Geynius*: and *Hondius* in one of his large Maps of *Asia*, does give another conjectural description of the like Chariots used in *China*.

Epig. 20. & 21.

The form of it is related to be very simple and plain, after this manner:

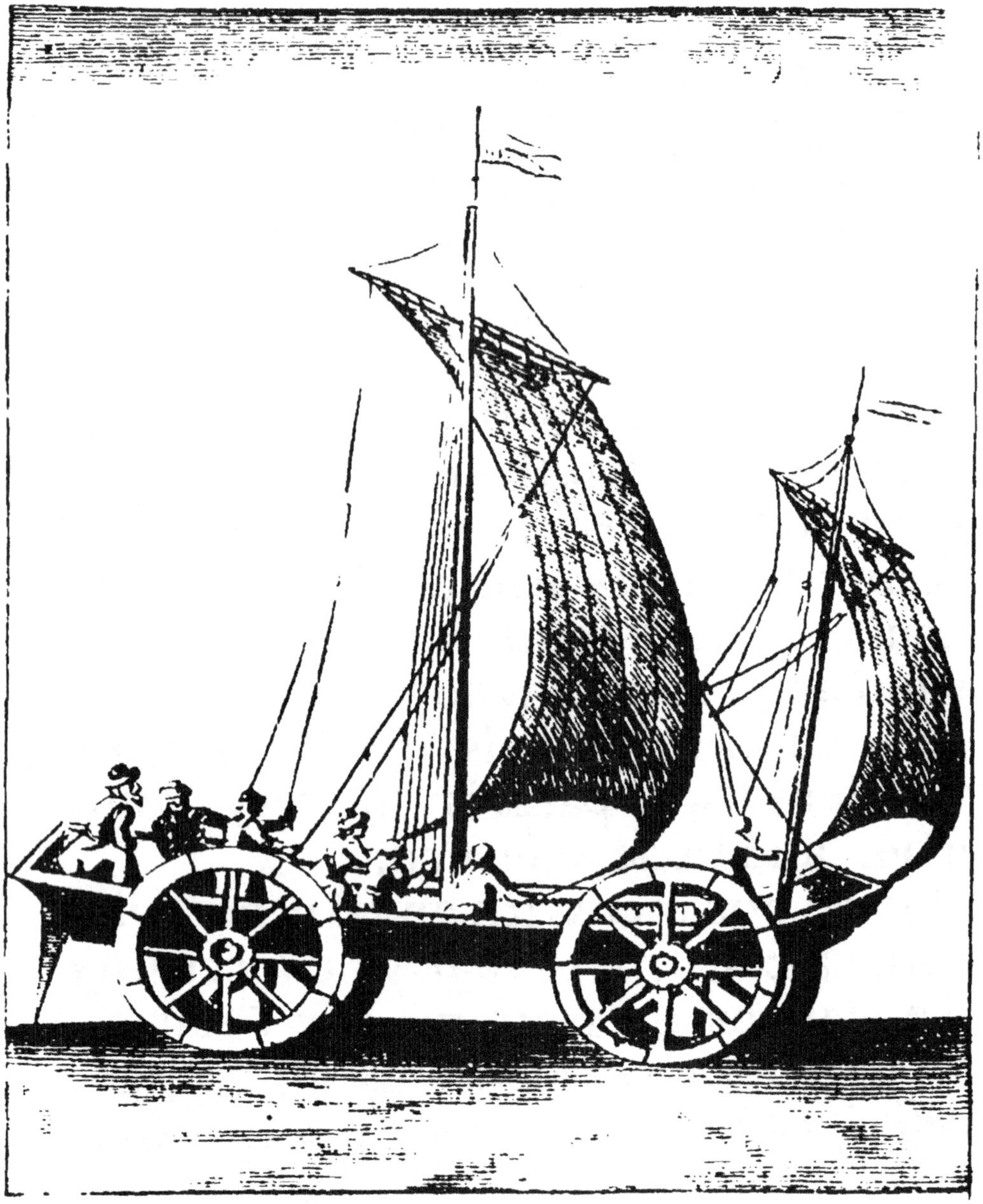

Cap. 2. *Mechanical Motions.*

The body of it being somewhat like a boat, moving upon 4 wheels of an equal bigness, with two sails like those in a ship; there being some contrivance to turn and steer it by moving a rudder which is placed beyond the two hindmost wheels: and for the stopping of it this must be done either by letting down the sail, or turning it from the wind. Of this kind they have frequently in *Holland* other little Vessels for one or two persons to go upon the ice, having sledges instead of wheels, being driven with a sail; the bodies of them like little boats, that if the ice should break, they might yet safely carry a man upon the water, where the sail would be stil useful for the motion of it.

I have often thought that it would be worth the experiment to enquire, whether or no such a sailing Chariot might not be more conveniently framed with moveable sails, whose force may be imprest from their motion, equivalent to those in a Wind-mill. Their foremost wheels (as in other Chariots) for the greater facility, being somewhat lower than the other, answerable to this fig.

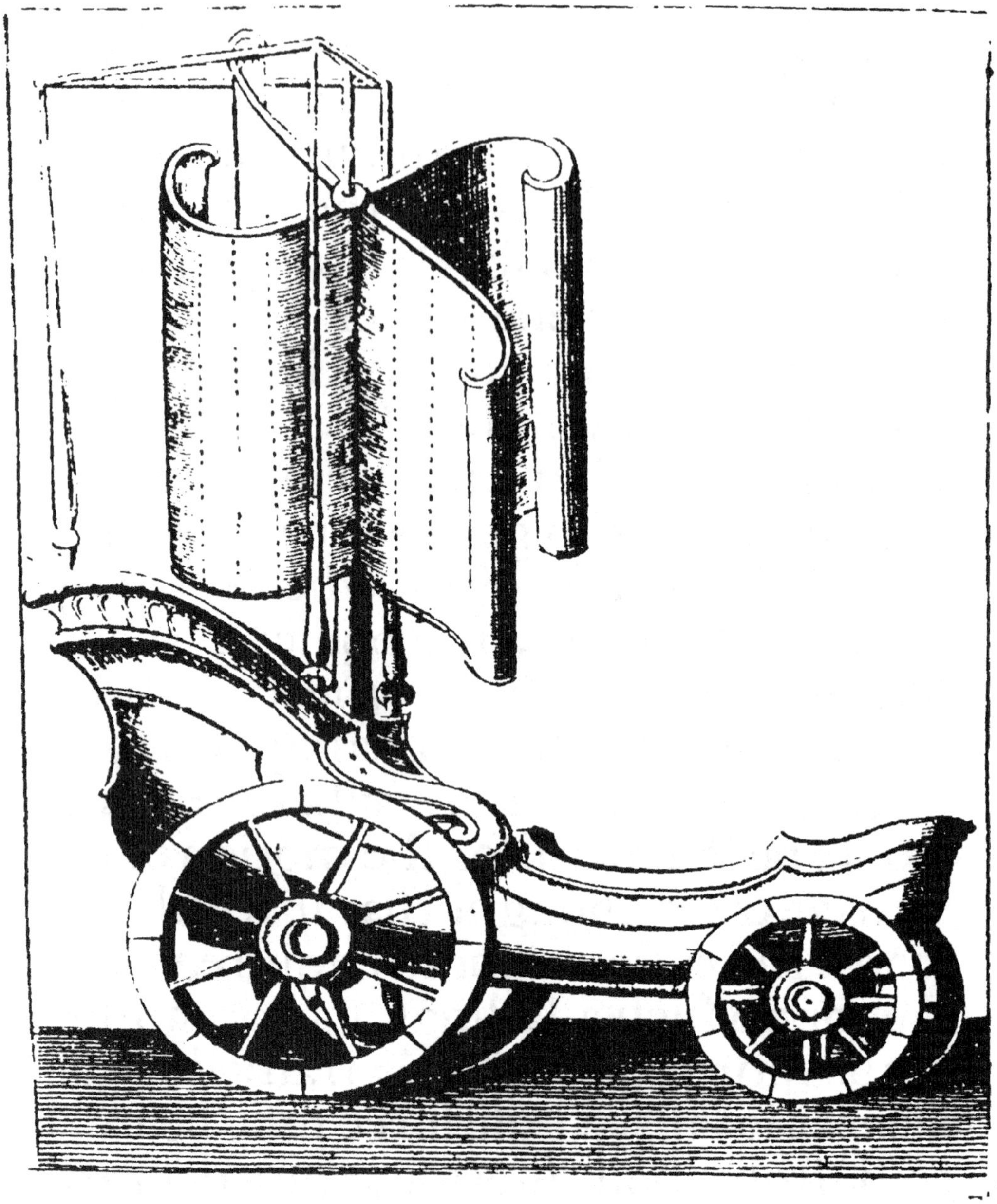

Cap. 2. *Mechanical Motions.*

In which the sails are so contrived, that the wind from any Coast will have a force upon them to turn them about, and the motion of these sails must needs turn the wheels, and consequently carry on the Chariot it self to any place (though fully against the wind) whither it shall be directed.

The chief doubt will be, whether in such a contrivance every little ruggedness or unevenness of the ground, will not cause such a jolting of the Chariot as to hinder the motion of its sails. But this perhaps (if it should prove so) is capable of several remedies.

I have often wondred, why none of our Gentry who live near great Plains, and smooth Champains, have attempted any thing to this purpose. The experiments of this kind being very pleasant, and not costly. What could be more delightful or better husbandry, than to make use of the *wind* (which costs nothing, and eats nothing) instead of *horses*? This being very easie to be effected by those, the convenience of whose habitations doth accommodate them for such experiments.

CAP. III.

Concerning the fixed Automata, Clocks, Spheres, *representing the heavenly motions: The several excellencies that are most commendable in such kind of contrivances*

THE second kind of ἀυτόματα were described to be such Engines, as did receive a regular and lasting motion from something belonging to their own frame, whether weights, or springs, &c.

They are usually distinguished into ἀυτόματα,

{ ϛᾶτα, fixed and stationary.
{ ὑπάρoντα, movable and transient.

1. The fixed are such as move only according to their several parts, and not according to their whole frame; In which, though each wheel hath a distinct rotation, yet the whole doth still remain unmoved. The chiefest kind

kind of these are the Clocks and Watches in ordinary use, the framing of which is so commonly known by every Mechanick, that I shall not trouble the Reader with any explication of it. He that desires fuller satisfaction, may see them particularly described by * *Cardan*, † D. *Flood*, and others.

* De variet. Rer. l. 9. c. 47.
† Tract. 2. part 7. l. 1. cap. 4. Repert. tit. 10. Architect. l. 10. c. 14.

The first invention of these (saith *Pancirollus*) was taken from that experiment in the multiplication of wheels mentioned in *Vitruvius*, where he speaks of an instrument whereby a man may know how many miles or paces he doth go in any space of time; whether or no he do pass by water in a boat or ship, or by land in a Chariot or Coach: they have been contrived also into little pocket-instruments, by which after a man hath walked a whole day together, he may easily know how many steps he hath taken. I forbear to enter upon a larger explication of these kind of Engines, because they are impertinent unto the chief business that

I have proposed for this discourse. The Reader may see them more particulary described in the above-cited place of *Vitruvius*, in * *Cardan.* † *Bessonius*, and others; I have here only mentioned them, as being the first occasion of the chiefest αὐτόματα that are now in use.

> * Subtil.
> † Theatrum instrumentorum. Weeker de secret. l. 15. c. 32.

Of the same kind with our Clocks and Watches (though perhaps more elaborate and subtil) was that sphere invented by *Archimedes*, which did represent the heavenly motions: the diurnal and annual courses of the Sun, the changes and aspects of the Moon, &c. This is frequently celebrated in the writings of the Ancients, particularly in that known *Epigram* of *Claudian*:

> Mentioned by Cicero. Tuscul. Quæst. l. 1. item De Nat. Deorum l. 2.

Jupiter in parvo cum cerneret æthera vitro,
  Risit, & ad Superos talia dicta dedit;
Huccine mortalis progressa potentia curæ?
  Jam mens in fragili luditur orbe labor.
Jura poli, rerumque fidem, legesque Deorum,
  Ecce Syracusius transtulit arte senex.
Inclusus variis famulatur * spiritus astris,
  Et vivum certis motibus urget opus.

> * The secret force from which the motion was impressed.

Per-

Cap. 3. *Mechanical Motions.*

Percurrit proprium mentitus Signifer annum;
 Et simulata novo Cynthia mense redit.
Jamq; suum volvens audax industria mundũ
 Gaudet & humana sidera mente regit.
Quid falso insontem tonitru Salmonea miror?
 Æmula naturæ parva reperta manus.

Excellently Translated by
T. Randolph.

Jove saw the heavens fram'd in a litle Glass,
And laughing, to the gods these words did pass;
Comes then the power of mortal cares so far?
In brittle Orbs my labours acted are.
The statutes of the Poles, the faith of things,
The laws of Gods, this Syracusian *brings*
Hither by art; Spirits inclos'd attend
Their several spheres, and with set motions bend
The living work; each year the feigned Sun,
Each month returns the counterfeited Moon.
And viewing now her world, bold industry
Grows proud, to know the heavens his subjects be.
Believe, Salmoneus *hath false thunders thrown,*
For a poor hand is natures rival grown.

But that this Engine should be made of glass, is scarce credible. *Lactantius* mentioning the relation of it, affirms it to consist of brass, which is more likely. It may be the outside or case was glass, and the frame it self of brass. *Cælius Rhodoginus,* speaking of the wonderous art in the contrivance

Instit.l.2. c. 5.

Antiq. est l. 2. c. 16.

of this sphere, breaks out into this quære, *Nonne igitur miraculorum omnium maximum miraculum est homo?* He might have said *Mathematicus*: And another to this purpose, *Sic manus ejus naturam, ut natura ipsa manum imitata putetur.* *Pappus* tells us, that *Archimedes* writ a Book *de Sphæropœia*, concerning the manner of framing such Engines; and after him *Posidonius* composed another discourse on the same subject, though now either the ignorance or the envy of time hath deprived us of both those works. And yet the art it self is not quite perished; for we read of divers the like contrivances in these latter times. *Agrippa* affirms, that he himself had seen such a sphere; & *Ramus* tels us how he beheld two of them in *Paris*, the one brought thither amongst other spoils from *Sicily*, and the other out of *Germany*. And it is commonly reported, that there is yet such a sphere at *Strasburgh* in *Germany*. * *Rivaltus* relates how *Marinus Burgesius*, a *Norman*, made two of them in *France* for the King.
And

And perhaps these latter (saith he) were more exact than the former, because the heavenly revolutions are now much better understood than before. And besides, it is questionable, whether the use of steel-springs was known in those ancient times; the application of which unto these kind of spheres, must needs be much more convenient than weights.

'Tis related also of the Consul *Boethius*, that amongst other Mathematical contrivances, (for which he was famous) he made a sphere to represent the Suns motion, which was so much admired, and talked of in those times, that *Gundibaldus* King of *Burgundy*, did purposely send over Embassadors to *Theodoricus* the Emperor, with intreaties that he would be a means to procure one of these spheres from *Boethius*; the Emperor thinking hereby to make his Kingdom more famous and terrible unto foreign Nations, doth write an Epistle to *Boethius*, perswading him to send this instrument. *Quoties non sunt credituri quod*

Cassiodor: Chron. Pet. Bertius. Præf. ad Consolat. Philos.

quod viderint? Quoties hanc veritatem lusoria somnia putabunt? Et quando fuerint à stupore conversi, non audebunt se æquales nobis dicere, apud quos sciunt sapientes talia cogitasse. So much were all these kind of inventions admired in those ruder and darker times; whereas the instruments that are now in use amongst us (though not so much extolled) yet do altogether equal (if not exceed) the other both in usefulness and subtilty. The chiefest of these former Engines receiving their motion from weights, and not from springs, which (as I said before) are of later and more excellent invention.

Polyd. Virgil. de invent. rerum l. 2. c. 5. Cardan. Subtil. l. 17.

The particular circumstances for which the *Automata* of this kind are most eminent, may be reduced to these four.

1. The lastingness of their motion, without needing any new supply; for which purpose there have been some Watches contrived to continue without winding up for a week together, or longer.

2. The

Cap. 3. *Mechanical Motions.*

2. The easiness and simplicity of their composition; Art it self being but the facilitating and contracting of ordinary operations; therefore the more easie and compendious such inventions are, the more artificial should they be esteemed. And the addition of any such unnecessary parts, as may be supplied some other way, is a sure sign of unskilfulness and ignorance. Those antiquated Engines that did consist of such a needless multitude of wheels, and springs, and screws, (like the old *hypothesis* of the heavens) may be compared to the notions of a confused knowledg, which are always full of perplexity and complications, and seldom in order; whereas the inventions of Art are more regular, simple and perspicuous, like the apprehensions of a distinct and thoroughly informed judgment. In this respect the manner of framing the ordinary *Automata*, hath been much bettered in these latter times above the former, and shall hereafter perhaps be yet more advantaged.
These

These kind of experiments (like all other humane arts) receiving additions from every days experiment.

To this purpose there is an invention consisting only of one hollow orb or wheel, whereby the hours may be as truly distinguished, as by any ordinary clock or watch. This wheel should be divided into several cavities, through each of which successively either sand or water must be contrived to pass, the heaviness of these bodies (being always in the ascending side of the wheel) must be counterpoised by a plummet that may be fastned about the pulley on the axis: this plummet will leisurely descend, according as the sand by running out of one cavity into the next, doth make the several parts of the wheel lighter or heavier, and so consequently there will be produced an equal and lasting motion, which may be easily applied to the distinction of hours.

3. The multitude and variety of those services for which they may be

Cap. 3. *Mechanical Motions.*

be useful. Unto this kind may we refer those Watches, by which a man may tell not only the hour of the day, but the minute of the hour, the day of the month, the age and aspects of the Moon, &c. Of this nature likewise was the Larum mentioned by *Walchius*, which though it were but two or three inches big, yet would both wake a man, and of it self light a candle for him at any set hour of the night. And those weights or springs which are of so great force as to turn a Mill, (as some have been contrived) may be easily applied to more various and difficult labours.

Fab. 9.

Ramel fig. 130.

4. The littleness of their frame. *Nunquam ars magis quàm in minimis nota est* (saith *Aquinas*). The smalness of the Engine doth much commend the skill of the artificer; to this purpose there have been Watches contrived in the form and quantity of a Jewel for the ear, where the striking of the minutes may constantly whisper unto us, how our lives do slide away

Jacks no bigger than a walnut, to turn any joint of meat.

172 *Dædalus; or,* Lib. II.

De subtil. l. 2. item l. 17.

away by a swift succession. *Cardan* tells us of a Smith who made a Watch in the Jewel of a ring, to be worn on the finger, which did shew the hours, (*non solum sagittâ, sed ictu*) not only by the hand, but by the finger too (as I may say) by pricking it every hour.

CAP. IV.

Of the movable and Gradient Automata, representing the motions of living creatures, various sounds of birds, or beasts, and some of them articulate.

THus much of those Automata, which were said to be fixed and stationary.

The other kind to be enquired after, are those that are movable and transient, which are described to be such engines as move not only according to their several parts, but also according to their whole frames. These are again distinguishable into two sorts:

1. *Gra-*

Cap. 4. *Mechanical Motions.*

1. *Gradient.*
2. *Volant.*

1. The *Gradient* or *ambulatory*, are such as require some *basis* or bottom to uphold them in their motions. Such were those strange inventions (commonly attributed to *Dædalus*) or self-moving statues, which (unless they were violently detained) would of themselves run away. * *Aristotle* affirms, that *Dædalus* did this by putting quick silver into them. But this would have been too gross a way for so excellent an Artificer; it is more likely that he did it with wheels and weights. Of this kind likewise were *Vulcans Tripodes*, celebrated by *Homer*, that were made to move up and down the house, and fight with one another. He might as well have contrived them into Journey-men statues, each of which with a hammer in his hand should have worked at the forge.

But amongst these fighting images, that in *Cardan* may deserve a mention, which holding in its hand a golden apple, beautified with many costly Jewels;

Plato in Menone. Arist. Polit. l. 1. c. 3.

* De Anima l. 1. c. 3.

Iliad. 18. There have been also chariots driven by the force of a spring contrived within them. De Variet. rerum. l. 12. c. 58.

Jewels; if any man offered to take it, the statue presently shot him to death. The touching of this apple serving to discharge several short bows, or other the like instruments that were secretly couched within the body of the image. By such a treachery was King *Chennetus* murdered (as *Boethius* relates).

It is so common an experiment in these times to represent the persons and actions of any story by such self-moving images, that I shall not need to explain the manner how the wheels and springs are contrived within them.

Amongst these gradient *Automata*, that Iron Spider mentioned in *Walchius*, is more especially remarkable, which being but of an ordinary bigness, besides the outward similitude, (which was very exact) had the same kind of motions with a living spider, and did creep up and down as if it had been alive. It must needs argue a wonderful art, and accurateness, to contrive all the instruments requisite for such a mo-

Fab. 9. There have been other inventions to move on the water. Navigium sponte mobile, ac sui remigii autorem faciam nullo negotio, saith Scaliger, Exerc. 326.

Cap. 3. *Mechanical Motions.*

a motion in so small a frame.

There have been also other motions contrived from Magnetical qualities, which will shew the more wonderful, because there is no apparent reason of their motion, there being not the least contiguity or dependance upon any other body that may occasion it; but it is all one as if they should move up and down in the open air. Get a glass sphere, fill it with such liquors as may be clear of the same colour, immixable, such as are oyl of Tartar, and spirit of wine: In which, it is easie so to poise a little globe or other statue, that it shall swim in the center. Under this glass sphere, there should be a Loadstone concealed, by the motion of which, the statue (having a needle touched within it) will move up and down, and may be contrived to shew the hour or sign. See several inventions of this kind in *Kircher de Arte Magnetica, L. 2.*

There have been some artificial images, which besides their several postures in walking up and down,
have

have been made also to give several sounds, whether of birds, as Larks Cuckooes, &c. or beasts, as Hares, Foxes. The voices of which creatures shall be rendered as clearly and distinctly, by these artificial images, as they are by those natural living bodies, which they represent.

There have been some inventions also which have been able for the utterance of articulate sounds, as the speaking of certain words. Such are some of the *Egyptian* Idols related to be. Such was the brazen head made by Fryar *Bacon*, and that statue in the framing of which *Albertus Magnus* bestowed thirty years, broken by *Aquinas*, who came to see it, purposely that he might boast, how in one minute he had ruined the labour of so many years.

Cœl. Rhod. lect. Ant. l. 2. c. 17. Maiolus Colloq.

Now the ground and reason how these sounds were contrived, may be worth our inquiry.

First then, for those of birds or beasts, they were made from such pipes or calls, as may express the several

veral tones of those creatures which are represented: these calls are so commonly known and used, that they need not any further explication.

But now about articulate sounds there is much greater difficulty. *Walchius* thinks it possible entirely to preserve the voice, or any words spoken, in a hollow trunk, or pipe, and that this pipe being rightly opened, the words will come out of it in the same order wherein they were spoken. Somewhat like that cold Countrey, where the peoples discourse doth freeze in the air all winter, and may be heard in the next Summer, or at a great thaw. But this conjecture will need no refutation.

Fab. 9.

The more substantial way for such a discovery, is by marking how nature her self doth employ the several instruments of speech, the tongue, lips, throat, teeth, &c. to this purpose the Hebrews have assigned each letter unto its proper instrument. And besides, we should observe what inarticulate sounds do resemble any of the

the particular letters. Thus we may note the trembling of water to be like the letter *L*, the quenching of hot things to the letter *Z*, the sound of strings, unto the letter *Ng*, the jirking of a switch the letter *Q*, &c. By an exact observation of these particulars, it is (perhaps) possible to make a statue speak some words.

Bacon Nat. Hist. Exper. 199 200.

CAP. V.

Concerning the possibility of framing an Ark for submarine Navigation. The difficulties and conveniences of such a contrivance.

IT will not be altogether impertinent unto the discourse of these gradient *Automata*, to mention what *Mersennus* doth so largely and pleasantly descant upon, concerning the making of a ship, wherein men may safely swim under water.

That such a contrivance is feasible and may be effected, is beyond all question, because it hath been already

Tract. de Magnetis proprietatibus.

dy experimented here in *England* by *Cornelius Dreble*; but how to improve it unto publick use and advantage, so as to be serviceable for remote voyages, the carrying of any confiderable number of men, with provisions and commodities, would be of such excellent use as may deserve some further inquiry.

Concerning which there are two things chiefly confiderable:

The { many difficulties with their remedies.
great conveniences.

1. The difficulties are generally reducible to these three heads.

1. The letting out, or receiving in any thing, as there shall be occasion, without the admission of water. If it have not such a convenience, these kind of voyages must needs be very dangerous and uncomfortable, both by reason of many noisom offensive things, which should be thrust out, and many other needful things, which should be received in. Now herein will confift the difficulty, how to contrive

trive the opening of this Vessel so, that any thing may be put in or out, and yet the water not rush into it with much violence, as it doth usually in the leak of a ship.

In which case this may be a proper remedy; let there be certain leather bags made of several bignesses, which for the *matter* of them should be both *tractable* for the use and managing of them, and *strong* to keep out the water; for the *figure* of them, being long and open at both ends. Answerable to these, let there be divers windows, or open places in the frame of the ship, round the sides of which one end of these bags may be fixed, the other end coming within the ship being to open and shut as a purse. Now if we suppose this bag thus fastned, to be tyed close about towards the window, then any thing that is to be sent out, may be safely put into that end within the ship, which being again close shut, and the other end loosened, the thing may be safely sent out without the admission of any water.

So

So again, when any thing is to be taken in, it muſt be firſt received into that part of the bag towards the window, which being (after the thing is within it) cloſe tyed about, the other end may then be ſafely opened. It is eaſie to conceive, how by this means any thing or perſon may be ſent out, or received in, as there ſhall be occaſion; how the water, which will perhaps by degrees leak into ſeveral parts, may be emptied out again, with divers the like advantages. Though if there ſhould be any leak at the bottom of the Veſſel, yet very little water would get in, becauſe no air could get out.

2. The ſecond difficulty in ſuch an Ark will be the *motion* or *fixing* of it according to occaſion; The *directing* of it to ſeveral places, as the voyage ſhall be deſigned, without which it would be very uſeleſs, if it were to remain only in one place, or were to remove only blindfold, without any certain direction; And the contrivance of this may ſeem very difficult,

cult; becaufe thefe fubmarine Navigators will want the ufual advantages of winds and tides for motion, and the fight of the heavens for direction.

But thefe difficulties may be thus remedied; As for the *progreffive* motion of it, this may be effected by the help of feveral Oars, which in the outward ends of them, fhall be like the fins of a fifh to contract and dilate. The paffage where they are admitted into the fhip being tyed about with fuch Leather bags (as were mentioned before) to keep out the water. It will not be convenient perhaps that the motion in thefe voyages fhould be very fwift, becaufe of thofe obfervations and difcoveries to be made at the bottom of the Sea, which in a little fpace may abundantly recompence the flownefs of its progrefs.

If this Ark be fo ballaft as to be of equal weight with the like magnitude of water, it will then be eafily movable in any part of it.

As for the *afcent* of it, this may be eafily contrived, if there be fome great weight

Cap. 5. *Mechanical Motions.*

weight at the bottom of the ship (being part of its ballast) which by some cord within may be loosned from it; As this weight is let lower, so will the ship ascend from it (if need be) to the very surface of the water; and again, as it is pulled close to the ship, so will it *descend*.

For *direction* of this Ark, the Mariners needle may be useful in respect of the *latitude* of places; and the course of this ship being more regular than others, by reason it is not subject to Tempests or unequal winds, may more certainly guide them in judging of the *longitude* of places.

3. But the greatest difficulty of all will be this, how the air may be supplied for respiration: How constant fires may be kept in it for light, and the dressing of food; how those vicissitudes of rarefaction and condensation may be maintained.

It is observed, that a barrel or cap, whose cavity will contain eight cubical feet of air, will not serve a Urinator or Diver for respiration, above

bove one quarter of an hour; the breath which is often sucked in and out, being so corrupted by the mixture of vapours, that Nature rejects it as unserviceable. Now in an hour a man will need at least 360 respirations, betwixt every one of which there shall be 10 second minutes, and consequently a great change and supply of air will be necessary for many persons, and any long space.

And so likewise for the keeping of fire; a close Vessel containing ten cubical feet of air, will not suffer a wax candle of an ounce to burn in it above an hour before it be suffocated, though this proportion (saith *Mersennus*) doth not equally increase for several lights, because four flames of an equal magnitude will be kept alive the space of 16 second minutes, though one of these flames alone in the same Vessel will not last above 25, or at most 30 seconds, which may be easily tried in large glass bottles, having wax candles lighted in them, and with their mouths inverted in water.
For

Cap. 5. *Mechanical Motions.*

For the rosolution of this difficulty, though I will not say that a man may by cuſtome (which in other things doth produce ſuch ſtrange incredible effects) be inabled to live in the open water as the fiſhes do, the inſpiration and expiration of water ſerving inſtead of air, this being uſual with many fiſhes that have lungs; yet it is certain that long uſe and cuſtome may ſtrengthen men againſt many ſuch inconveniences of this kind, which to unexperienced perſons may prove very hazardous: and ſo it will not perhaps be unto theſe ſo neceſſary, to have the air for breathing ſo pure and defecated as is required for others.

But further, there are in this caſe theſe three things conſiderable.

1. That the Veſſel it ſelf ſhould be of a large capacity, that as the air in it is corrupted in one part, ſo it may be purified and renewed in the other: or if the meer refrigeration of the air would fit it for breathing, this might be ſomewhat helped with bellows,

bellows, which would cool it by motion.

2. It is not altogether improbable, that the lamps or fires in the middle of it, like the reflected beams in the first Region, Rarefying the air, and the circumambient coldness towards the sides of the Vessel, like the second Region, cooling and condensing of it, would make such a vicissitude and change of air, as might fit it for all its proper uses.

3. Or if neither of these conjectures will help, yet *Mersennus* tells us in another place, that there is in *France* one *Barricus* a Diver, who hath lately found out another art, whereby a man might easily continue under water for six hours together; and whereas ten cubical feet of air will not serve another Diver to breathe in, for half an hour, he by the help of a cavity, not above one or two foot at most, will have breath enough for six hours, and a lanthorn scarce above the usual size to keep a candle burning as long as a man please, which

(if

Harmon. l.4.prop.6. Monit.

Cap. 5. *Mechanical Motions.*

(if it be true, and were commonly known) might be a sufficient help against this greatest difficulty.

As for the many advantages and conveniences of such a contrivance, it is not easie to recite them.

1. 'Tis *private*; a man may thus go to any coast of the world invisibly, without being discovered or prevented in his journey.

2. 'Tis *safe*; from the uncertainty of *Tides*, and the violence of *Tempests*, which do never move the sea above five or six paces deep. From *Pirates* and *Robbers* which do so infest other voyages; from ice and great frosts, which do so much endanger the passages towards the Poles.

3. It may be of very great advantage against a Navy of enemies, who by this means may be undermined in the water, and blown up.

4. It may be of a special use for the relief of any place that is besieged by water, to convey unto them invisible supplies: and so likewise for the surprisal of any place that is accessible by water.

5. It may be of unspeakable benefit for submarine experiments and discoveries: as,

The several proportions of swiftness betwixt the ascent of a bladder, cork, or any other light substance, in comparison to the descent of stones or lead. The deep caverns and subterraneous passages where the sea-water in the course of its circulation, doth vent it self into other places, and the like. The nature and kinds of fishes, the several arts of catching them, by alluring them with lights, by placing divers nets about the sides of this Vessel, shooting the greater sort of them with guns, which may be put out of the ship by the help of such bags as were mentioned before, with divers the like artifices and treacheries, which may be more successively practised by such who live so familiarly together. These fish may serve not only for food, but for fewel likewise, in respect of that oyl which may be extracted from them; the way of dressing meat by lamps, being

ing in many respects the most convenient for such a voyage.

The many fresh springs that may probably be met with in the bottom of the sea, will serve for the supply of drink and other occasions.

But above all, the discovery of submarine treasures is more especially considerable, not only in regard of what hath been drowned by wrecks, but the several precious things that grow there, as Pearl, Coral Mines, with innumerable other things of great value, which may be much more easily found out, and fetcht up by the help of this, than by any other usual way of the Urinators.

To which purpose, this great Vessel may have some lesser Cabins tyed about it, at various distances, wherein several persons, as Scouts, may be lodged for the taking of observations, according as the Admiral shall direct them. Some of them being frequently sent up to the surface of the water, as there shall be occasion.

All

All kind of arts and manufactures may be exercised in this Vessel. The observations made by it, may be both written and (if need were) printed here likewise. Several Colonies may thus inhabit, having their Children born and bred up without the knowledg of land, who could not chuse but be amazed with strange conceits upon the discovery of this upper world.

I am not able to judge what other advantages there may be suggested, or whether experiment would fully answer to these notional conjectures. But however, because the invention did unto me seem ingenious and new, being not impertinent to the present enquiry, therefore I thought it might be worth the mentioning.

C A P.

CAP. VI.

Of the volant Automata, Archytas *his Dove, and* Regiomontanus *his Eagle. The possibility and great usefulness of such inventions.*

THE *volant* or flying *Automata*, are such Mechanical contrivances, as have a self-motion, whereby they are carried aloft in the open air, like the flight of Birds. Such was that wooden Dove made by *Archytas*, a Citizen of *Tarentum*, and one of *Plato*'s acquaintance. And that wooden Eagle framed by *Regiomontanus* at *Noremberg*, which by way of triumph, did fly out of the City to meet *Charles* the fifth. This later Author is also reported to have made an iron Fly, *Quæ ex artificis manu egressa, convivas circumvolitavit, tandemque veluti defessa in Domini manus reversa est*, which when he invited any of his friends, would fly to each of them round the table, and at length (as being weary) return unto its Master.

Diog. Laer. l. 8.
Pet. Crinitus de honest. disci. l. 17. c. 12.

Ramus Schol. Mathem. l. 2.

Dubartas, 6 days 1 w.
J. Dee Preface to Euclid.

Cardan

Cardan seems to doubt the possibility of any such contrivance; his reason is, because the instruments of it must be firm and strong, and consequently they will be too heavy to be carried by their own force; but yet (saith he) if it be a little helped in the first rising; and if there be any wind to assist it in the flight, then there is nothing to hinder, but that such motions may be possible. So that he doth in effect grant as much as may be sufficient for the truth and credit of those ancient relations; and to distrust them without a stronger argument, must needs argue a blind and perverse incredulity. As for his objection concerning the heaviness of the materials in such an invention, it may be answered, That it is easie to contrive such springs and other instruments, whose strength shall much exceed their heaviness. Nor can he shew any cause why these Mechanical motions may not be as strong, (though not so lasting) as the natural strength of living creatures.

Scaliger

De Variet. rerum lib. 12. c. 58.

Cap. 6. *Mechanical Motions.*

Scaliger conceives the framing of such volant *Automata*, to be very easie. *Volantis columbæ machinulam, cujus autorem Archytam tradunt, vel facillimè profiteri audeo.* Those ancient motions were thought to be contrived by the force of some included air: So *Gellius Ita erat scilicet libramentis suspensum, & aurâ spiritus inclusâ atque occulta consitum, &c.* As if there had been some lamp, or other fire within it, which might produce such a forcible rarefaction, as should give a motion to the whole frame.

But this may be better performed by the strength of some such spring as is commonly used in Watches; this spring may be applied unto one wheel, which shall give an equal motion to both the wings; these wings having unto each of them another smaller spring by which they may be contracted and lifted up: So that being forcibly depressed by the strength of the great and stronger spring, and lifted up again by the other two; according to this suppo-

Subtil. Exercit. 326.

Noct. Attic. l. 10. cap. 12 where he thinks it so strange an invention that he styles Res abhorrens à fide Athan. Kircher de Magnete l. 2 par. 4. Poem. doth promise a large discourse concerning these kind of inventions in another Treatise which he styles Oedipus Ægyptiacus.

sition, it is easie to conceive how the motion of flight may be performed and continued.

The wings may be made either of *several substances joyned*, like the feathers in ordinary fowl, as *Dædalus* is feigned to contrive them, according to that in the Poet,

Ovid. Metam. l. 8.

> *--Ignotas animum dimittit in artes,*
> *Naturamque novat, nam ponit in ordine pennas*
> *A minimo cœptas longam breviore sequente,*
> *Ut clivo crevisse putes, &c.*

Or else of *one continuate substance*, like those of Bats. In framing of both which, the best guidance is to follow (as near as may be) the direction of nature; this being but an imitation of a natural work. Now in both these, the strength of each part is proportioned to the force of its imployment. But nothing in this kind can be perfectly determined without a particular trial.

Though the composing of such motions may be a sufficient reward to any ones industry in the searching

Cap. 6. *Mechanical Motions.*

after them, as being in themselves of excellent curiosity; yet there are some other inventions depend upon them, of more general benefit and greater importance. For if there be any such artificial contrivances that can fly in the air, (as is evident from the former relations, together with the grounds here specified, and I doubt not, may be easily effected by a diligent and ingenious artificer) then it will clearly follow, that it is possible also for a man to fly himself: It being easie from the same grounds to frame an instrument, wherein any one may sit, and give such a motion unto it as shall convey him aloft through the air. Than which there is not any imaginable invention that could prove of greater benefit to the world, or glory to the Author   And therefore it may justly deserve their enquiry, who have both leisure and means for such experiments.

But in these practical studies, unless a man be able to go to the tryal of things, he will perform but little.

little. In such matters,

—Studium sine divite venâ,   *Horace.*

(as the Poet saith) a general speculation, without particular experiment, may conjecture at many things, but can certainly effect nothing. And therefore I shall only propose unto the world, the Theory and general grounds that may conduce to the easie and more perfect discovery of the subject in question, for the encouragement of those that have both minds and means for such experiments. This same Scholars fate,

Res angusta domi, and
—curta supellex.

is that which hinders the promoting of learning in sundry particulars, and robs the world of many excellent inventions. We read of *Aristotle*, that he was allowed by his Pupil *Alexander* 800 talents a year, for the payment of Fishers, Fowlers, and Hunters, who were to bring him in several creatures, that so by his particular experience of their parts and dispositions, he might be more fitly prepared

Cap. 6. *Mechanical Motions.*

pared to write of their natures. The reason why the world hath not many *Aristotles* is, because it hath so few *Alexanders*.

Amongst other impediments of any strange invention or attempts, it is none of the meanest discouragements, that they are so generally derided by common opinion, being esteemed only as the dreams of a melancholy and distempered fancy. *Eusebius* speaking with what necessity every thing is confined by the laws of nature, and the decrees of providence, so that nothing can go out of that way, unto which naturally it is designed; as a fish cannot reside on the land, nor a man in the water, or aloft in the air, infers that therefore none will venture upon any such vain attempt, as passing in the air, ἢ μελαγχολίας ποιήματα ἂν περιπέσοι, unless his brain be a little crazed with the humour of melancholy; whereupon he advises that we should not in any particular endeavour to transgress the bounds of nature, ἐδὲ ἄπτερον ἔχοντα τὸ σῶμα, τὰ τ̃ πτη-

ContraHierocl. confut. l. 1.

πτηνῶν ἐπιτηδεύειν, and since we are naturally destitute of wings, not to imitate the flight of Birds. That saying of the Poet,

Demens qui nimbos & non imitabile fulmen, &c.

hath been an old censure applied unto such as ventured upon any strange or incredible attempt.

Hence may we conceive the reason, why there is so little intimation in the writings of antiquity, concerning the possibility of any such invention. The Ancients durst not so much as mention the art of flying, but in a fable.

Dædalus, ut fama est, fugiens Minoia regna,
Præpetibus pennis ausus se credere cælo,
Insuetum per iter gelidas enavit ad arctos, &c.

It was the custom of those former ages, in their overmuch gratitude, to advance the first Authors of any useful discovery, amongst the number of their gods. And *Dædalus* being so famous amongst them for sundry

[margin: Virgil. Æneid. l. 6.]

sundry Mechanical inventions (especially the sails of ships) though they did not for these place him in the heavens, yet they have promoted him as near as they could, feigning him to fly aloft in the air, when as he did but fly in a swift ship, as *Diodorus* relates the Historical truth, on which that fiction is grounded.

So Eusebius too.

CAP. VII.

Concerning the Art of flying. The several ways whereby this hath been, or may be attempted.

I Have formerly in two other * Discourses mentioned the possibility of this art of flying, and intimated a further inquiry unto it, which is a kind of engagement to some fuller disquisitions and conjectures to that purpose.

* World in the Moon, cap. 14. Mercury, or the secret and swift Messenger c. 4.

There are four several ways whereby this flying in the air, hath been or may be attempted. Two of them by the strength of other things, and two

two of them by our own strength.

1. By Spirits or Angels.
2. By the help of fowls.
3. By wings faſtned immediately to the body.
4. By a flying Chariot.

Zanch. de oper. pars 1. l. 4.

1. For the firſt, we read of divers that have paſſed ſwiftly in the air, by the help of Spirits and Angels, whether good Angels, as * *Elias* was carried into heaven in a fiery chariot: as † *Philip* was conveyed to *Azotus*, and *Habakkuk* from Jewry to Babylon, and back again immediately: Or by evil Angels, as our Saviour was carried by the Devil to the top of a high mountain, and to the pinacle of the Temple. Thus Witches are commonly related to paſs unto their uſual meetings in ſome remote place; and as they do ſell winds unto Mariners, ſo likewiſe are they ſometimes hired to carry men ſpeedily through the open air. *Acoſta* affirms, that ſuch kind of paſſages are uſual amongſt divers Sorcerers with the *Indians* at this day.

* *2 Kings 2. 11.*
† *Acts 8. 39. Dan. Apoc. 39.*

Luke 4.

Eraſtus de Lamiis.

Hiſt. Ind. l. 7. c. 26.

So

Cap. 7.　　*Mechanical Motions.*　　201

So *Kepler* in his Astronomical dream doth fancy a Witch to be conveyed unto the Moon by her Familiar.

Simon Magus was so eminent for miraculous Sorceries, that all the people in *Samaria*, from the least to the greatest, did esteem him *as the great power of God*. And so famous was he at *Rome*, that the Emperour erected a statue to him with this Inscription, *Simoni Deo Sancto*. 'Tis storied of this Magician, that having challenged Saint *Peter* to do Miracles with him, he attempted to fly from the Capitol to the Aventine Hill. But when he was in the midst of the way, Saint *Peters* prayers did overcome his Sorceries, and violently bring him to the ground, in which fall having broke his thigh, within a while after he dyed.

Acts 8. 10.

Hegesip. l. 3. c. 2. Pol. Virgil. de Inven. Rer. l. 8. c. 3. Pet. Crinitus de Honestâ Disciplin. l. 8: c. 1. mistrusts this relation as fabulous. Non enim Lucas hoc omisisset.

But none of all these relations may conduce to the discovery of this experiment, as it is here enquired after, upon *natural* and *artificial* grounds.

2. There are others who have con-

conjectured a possibility of being conveyed through the air by the help of Fowls; to which purpose that fiction of the *Ganza*'s, is the most pleasant and probable. They are supposed to be great fowl of a strong lasting flight, and easily tamable. Divers of which may be so brought up, as to joyn together in carrying the weight of a man, so as each of them shall partake his proportionable share of the burden; and the person that is carried may by certain reins direct and steer them in their courses. However this may seem a strange proposal, yet it is not certainly more improbable, than many other arts, wherein the industry of ingenious men hath instructed these brute creatures. And I am very confident, that one whose genius doth enable him for such kind of experiments, upon leisure, and the advantage of such helps as are requisite for various and frequent trials, might effect some strange thing by this kind of enquiry.

'Tis reported as a custom amongst the

Cap. 7. *Mechanical Motions.*

the *Leucatians*, that they were wont upon a superstition to precipitate a man from some high cliff into the Sea, tying about him with strings at some distance, many great fowls, and fixing unto his body divers feathers spread to break the fall; which (saith the learned *Bacon*, if it were diligently and exactly contrived) would be able to hold up, and carry any proportionable weight; and therefore he advises others to think further upon this experiment, as giving some light to the invention of the art of flying.

Nat Hist. experim. 816.

3. 'Tis the more obvious and common opinion, that this may be effected by wings fastned immediately to the body, this coming nearest to the imitation of Nature, which should be observed in such attempts as these. This is that way which *Fredericus Hermannus* in his little discourse *de Arte volandi,* doth only mention and insist upon. And if we may trust credible story, it hath been frequently attempted, not without some success.

So the ancient British Bladuds.

'Tis

Ernestus Burgravus in Panoplia Physico-Vultania. Sturmius in Lat. linguæ resolut.

Melancholy. Part. 2. Sect. 1 Mem 3.

'Tis related of a certain English Monk called *Elmerus*, about the Confessor's time, that he did by such wings fly from a Tower above a furlong; and so another from Saint *Marks* steeple in *Venice*; another at *Norinberge*; and *Busbequius* speaks of a Turk in *Constantinople*, who attempted something this way. Mr. *Burton* mentioning this quotation, doth believe that some new-fangled wit ('tis his Cynical phrase) will some time or other find out this art. Though the truth is, most of these Artists did unfortunately miscarry by falling down and breaking their arms or legs, yet that may be imputed to their want of experience, and too much fear, which must needs possess men in such dangerous and strange attempts. Those things that seem very difficult and fearful at the first, may grow very facil after frequent trial and exercise. And therefore he that would effect any thing in this kind, must be brought up to the constant practice of it from his youth. Trying

Cap. 7. Mechanical Motions.

ing first only to use his wings in running on the ground, as an Estrich or tame Geese will do, touching the earth with his toes; and so by degrees learn to rise higher, till he shall attain unto skill and confidence. I have heard it from credible testimony, that one of our own Nation hath proceeded so far in this experiment, that he was able by the help of wings in such a running pace, to step constantly ten yards at a time.

It is not more incredible, that frequent practice and custom should inable a man for this, than for many other things which we see confirmed by experience. What strange agility and activeness do our common tumblers and dancers on the rope attain to by continual exercise? 'Tis related of certain *Indians*, that they are able when a horse is running in his full career, to stand upright on his back, to turn themselves round, to leap down, gathering up any thing from the ground, and immediately to leap up again, to shoot exactly at any mark, the horse not intermitting

Maffæus Hist Ind. l. 1.

termitting his courſe. And ſo upon two horſes together, the man ſetting one of his feet upon each of them. Theſe things may ſeem impoſſible to others, and it would be very dangerous for any one to attempt them, who hath not firſt gradually attained to theſe arts, by long practice and trial; and why may not ſuch practice enable him as well for this other experiment, as for theſe things?

There are others who have invented ways, to walk upon the water, as regularly and as firmly as upon the land. There are ſome ſo accuſtomed to this element, that it hath been almoſt as natural to them, as to the fiſh; men that could remain for above an hour together under water. *Pontanus* mentions one who could ſwim above a hundred miles together, from one ſhore to another, with great ſpeed, and at all times of the year. And it is ſtoried of a certain young man, a *Sicilian* by birth, and a *Diver* by profeſſion, who had ſo continually uſed himſelf to the water, that he could not

Treatiſe of cuſtom.

Cap. 7. *Mechanical Motions.*

not enjoy his health out of it. If at any time he staid with his friends on the land, he should be so tormented with a pain in his stomack, that he was forced for his health to return back again to Sea, wherein he kept his usual residence; and when he saw any ships, his custom was to swim to them for relief, which kind of life he continued till he was an old man, and dyed.

I mention these things, to shew the great power of practice and custom, which might more probably succeed in this experiment of flying (if it were but regularly attempted) than in such strange effects as these.

It is a usual practice in these times, for our *Funambulones*, or Dancers on the Rope, to attempt somewhat like to flying, when they will with their heads forwards slide down a long Cord extended; being fastned at one end on the top of some high Tower, and the other at some distance on the ground; with wings fixed to their shoulders, by the shaking of which
they

they will break the force of their descent. It would seem that some attempts of this kind were usually amongst the *Romans*. To which that expression in * *Salvian* may refer, where amongst other publick shews of the Theater, he mentions the *Petaminarii*: which word (saith *Jo. Brassicanus*) is scarce to be found in any other Author, being not mentioned either in *Julius Pollux*, or *Politian*. 'Tis probably derived from the Greek word πέτασθαι, which signifies to fly, and may refer to such kind of Rope-dancers.

*De gub. Dei l. 6.

Annot. in Salv.

But now because the arms extended are but weak and easily wearied, therefore the motions by them are like to be but short and slow, answerable it may be to the flight of such domestick fowl, as are most conversant on the ground, which of themselves we see are quickly weary, and therefore much more would the arm of a man, as being not naturally designed to such a motion.

It were therefore worth the inquiry

ry to consider whether this might not be more probably effected by the labour of the feet, which are naturally more strong and indefatigable: In which contrivance the wings should come down from the shoulders on each side as in the other, but the motion of them should be from the legs, being thrust out and drawn in again one after another, so as each leg should move both wings, by which means a man should (as it were) walk or climb up into the air: and then the hands and arms might be at leisure to help and direct the motion, or for any other service proportionable to their strength. Which conjecture is not without good probability, and some special advantages above the other.

4. But the fourth and last way seems unto me altogether as probable, and much more useful than any of the rest: And that is by a flying Chariot, which may be so contrived as to carry a man within it; and though the strength of a spring might per-

haps be serviceable for the motion of this engine, yet it were better to have it assisted by the labour of some intelligent mover, as the heavenly Orbs are supposed to be turned. And therefore if it were made big enough to carry sundry persons together, then each of them in their several turns might successively labour in the causing of this motion; which thereby would be much more constant and lasting, than it could otherwise be, if it did wholly depend on the strength of the same person. This contrivance being as much to be preferred before any of the other, as swimming in a ship before swimming in the water.

CHAP. VIII.

A resolution of the two chief difficulties that seem to oppose the possibility of a flying Chariot.

THE chief difficulties against the possibility of any such contrivance, may be fully removed in the resolution

Cap. 8. *Mechanical Motions.*

folution of thefe two *Quæries*.

1. Whether an engine of such capacity and weight, may be supported by so thin and light a body as the air?

2. Whether the strength of the persons within, it may be sufficient for the motion of it?

1. Concerning the first; when *Callias* was required by the men of *Rhodes*, to take up that great *Helepolis*, brought against them by *Demetrius*, (as he had done before unto some less, which he himself had made) He answered, that it could not be done. *Nonnulla enim sunt quæ in exemplaribus videntur similia, cum autem crescere cæperunt, dilabuntur.* Because those things that appear probable in lesser models, when they are encreased to a greater proportion, do thereby exceed the power of art. For example, though a man may make an instrument to bore a hole an inch wide, or half an inch, and so less; yet to bore a hole of a foot wide, or two foot, is not so much as to be

Vitruvius Archit. l. 10. c. 22.

So Ramus Schol. Mathem. l. 1.

P 2   thought

thought of. Thus though the air may be able to uphold some lesser bodies, as those of birds; yet when the quantity of them is encreased to any great extension, it may justly be doubted, whether they will not exceed the proportion that is naturally required unto such kind of bodies.

To this I answer, That the engine can never be too big or too heavy, if the space which it possesses in the air, and the motive-faculty in the instrument be answerable to its weight. That saying of *Callias* was but a groundless shift and evasion whereby he did endeavour to palliate his own ignorance and disability. The utmost truth which seems to be implied in it, is this: That there may be some bodies of so great a bigness, and gravity, that it is very difficult to apply so much force unto any particular instrument, as shall be able to move them.

Against the example, it may be affirmed and easily proved, that it is equally possible to bore a hole of any bigness,

bigness, as well great as little, if we suppose the instrument, and the strength, and the application of this strength to be proportionable; But because of the difficulty of these concurrent circumstances in those greater and more unusual operations, therefore do they falsly seem to be absolutely impossible.

So that the chief inference from this argument and example, doth imply only thus much, that it is very difficult to contrive any such motive power, as shall be answerable to the greatness and weight of such an instrument as is here discoursed of, which doth not at all impair the truth to be maintained; For if the possibility of such a motion be yeilded, we need not make any scruple of granting the difficulty of it; It is this must add a glory to the invention; and yet this will not perhaps seem so very difficult to any one who hath but diligently observed the flight of some other birds, particularly of a kite, how he will swim up and down in the air, sometimes at a great height, and presently again lower, guiding himself by his train, with his wings extended without any sensible motion of them; and all this when there is only some gentle breath of air stirring, without the help of any strong forcible wind. Now I say, if that fowl (which is none of the lightest) can so very easily move it self up and down in the air, without so much as stirring the wings of it; certainly then, it is not improbable, but that when all the due proportions in such an engine are found out, and when men by long practise have arrived to any skill and experience, they will be able in this (as well as in many other things) to come very near unto the imitation of nature.

Sen. Nat. Qu. l. 3. s. 25.

As it is in those bodies which are carried on the water, though they be never so big, or so ponderous, (suppose equal to a City or a whole Island) yet they will always swim on the top, if they be but any thing lighter than so much water

as

as is equal to them in bigness: So likewise is it in the bodies that are carried in the air. It is not their greatness (though never so immense) that can hinder their being supported in that light element, if we suppose them to be extended unto a proportionable space of air. And as from the former experiments, *Archimedes* hath composed a subtil *science* in his Book, *De insidentibus humido,* concerning the weight of any heavy body, in reference to the water wherein it is: So from the particular trial of these other experiments, that are here inquired after, it is possible to raise a new science, concerning the extension of bodies, in comparison to the air, and motive faculties by which they are to be carried.

We see a great difference betwixt the several quantities of such bodies as are commonly upheld by the air; not only little gnats, and flies, but also the Eagle and other fowl of vaster magnitude. *Cardan* and *Scaliger* do unanimously affirm, that there is a

bird

bird amongst the *Indians* of so great a bigness, that his beak is often used to make a sheath or scabbard for a sword. And *Acosta* tells us of a fowl in *Peru* called *Condores*, which will of themselves kill and eat up a whole Calf at a time. Nor is there any reason why any other body may not be supported and carried by the air, though it should as much exceed the quantity of these fowl, as they do the quantity of a fly.

Hystor. Nov. Orb. l. 4. c. 37.

Marcus Polus mentions a fowl in *Madagascar*, which he calls a *Ruck*, the feathers of whose wings are 12 paces, or threescore foot long, which can with as much ease soop up an Elephant, as our Kites do a Mouse. If this relation were any thing credible, it might serve as an abundant proof for the present quæry. But I conceive this to be already so evident, that it needs not any fable for its further confirmation.

2. The other doubt was, whether the strength of the other persons within it, will be sufficient for the moving

Cap. 8. *Mechanical Motions.*

moving of this engine? I answer, the main difficulty and labour of it will be in the raising of it from the ground; near unto which, the earths attractive vigor is of greatest efficacy. But for the better effecting of this, it may be helped by the strength of winds, and by taking its first rise from some mountain, or other high place. When once it is aloft in the air, the motion of it will be easie, as it is in the flight of all kind of birds, which being at any great distance from the earth, are able to continue their motion for a long time and way, with little labour or weariness.

'Tis certain from common relation and experience, that many birds do cross the seas for divers hundred miles together: sundry of them amongst us, which are of a short wing and flight, as Blackbirds, Nightingales, &c. do fly from us into *Germany*, and other remoter Countries. And Mariners do commonly affirm, that they have found some fowl above six hundred miles from any land.

Plin. l. 10. c. 23.

Now

Now if we should suppose these birds to labour so much in those long journeys, as they do when they fly in our sight, and near the earth, it were impossible for any of them to pass so far without resting. And therefore it is probable, that they do mount unto so high a place in the air, where the natural heaviness of their bodies does prove but little or no impediment to their flight; Though perhaps either hunger, or the sight of ships, or the like accident, may sometimes occasion their descending lower, as we may guess of those birds, which Mariners have thus beheld; and divers others, that have been drowned and cast up by the sea.

Whence it may appear, that the motion of this Chariot (though it may be difficult at the first) yet will still be easier, as it ascends higher, till at length it shall become utterly devoid of gravity, when the least strength will be able to bestow upon it a swift motion: as I have proved more

Cap. 8. *Mechanical Motions.*

more at large in another discourse.

But then, (may some object) If it be supposed that a man in the æthereal air does lose his own heaviness, how shall he contribute any force towards the motion of this instrument?

I answer, The strength of any living creature in these external motions, is something really distinct from, and superadded unto its natural gravity; as common experience may shew, not only in the impression of blows or violent motions, as a River-Hawk will strike a fowl with a far greater force, than the meer descent or heaviness of his body could possibly perform: But also in those actions which are done without such help, as the pinching of the finger, the biting of the teeth, &c. all which are of much greater strength than can proceed from the meer heaviness of those parts.

As for the other particular doubts, concerning the extreme thinness and coldness of this æthereal air, by reason of which it may seem to be al-

World in the Moon, c. 14.

altogether impassible, I have already resolved them in the above-cited discourse.

The uses of such a Chariot may be various; Besides the discoveries which might be thereby made in the Lunary world; It would be serviceable also for the conveyance of a man to any remote place of this earth: as suppose to the *Indies* or *Antipodes*. For when once it was elevated for some few miles, so as to be above that Orb of Magnetick virtue, which is carried about by the earths diurnal revolution, it might then be very easily and speedily directed to any particular place of this great Globe.

If the place which we intended were under the same parallel, why then the earths revolution once in twenty four hours, would bring it to be under us; so that it would be but descending in a streight line, and we might presently be there. If it were under any other parallel, it would then only require that we should direct it in the same Meridian, till we did come to

that

Cap. 8. *Mechanical Motions.*

that parallel; and then (as before) a man might easily descend unto it.

It would be one great advantage in this kind of travelling, that one should be perfectly freed from all inconveniences of ways or weather, not having any extremity of heat, or cold, or Tempests to molest him: This æthereal air being perpetually in an equal temper and calmness. *Pars superior mundi ordinatior est nec in nubem cogitur, nec in tempestatem impellitur, nec versatur in turbinem, omni tumultu caret, inferiora fulminant.* The upper parts of the world are always quiet and serene, no winds and blustring there; they are these lower cloudy regions that are so full of tempests and combustion.

Sen. de Irâ l. 3. c. 6. Pacem summa tenens. Lucan.

As for the manner how the force of a spring, or (instead of that) the strength of any living person, may be applied to the motion of these wings of the Chariot, it may easily be apprehended from what was formerly delivered.

There are divers other particulars

to be more fully enquired after, for the perfecting of such a flying Chariot; as concerning the proportion of the wings both for their length and breadth, in comparison to the weight which is to be carried by them, as also concerning those special contrivances, whereby the strength of these wings may be severally applied either to ascent, descent, progressive, or a turning motion; All which, and divers the like enquiries can only be resolved by particular experiments. We know the invention of sailing in ships does continually receive some new addition from the experience of every age, and hath been a long while growing up to that perfection, unto which it is now arrived. And so must it be expected for this likewise, which may at first perhaps seem perplexed with many difficulties and inconveniences, and yet upon the experience of frequent tryals, many things may be suggested to make it more facil and commodious.

As well too long as too short, too broad as too narrow, may be an impediment to the motion, by making it more difficult, slow and flaging

He

Cap. 8. *Mechanical Motions.*

He that would regularly attempt any thing to this purpose, should observe this progress in his experiments, he should first make enquiry what kind of wings would be most useful to this end; those of a Bat being most easily imitable, and perhaps nature did by them purposely intend some intimation to direct us in such experiments; that creature being not properly a bird, because not amongst the *Ovipara*, to imply that other kind of creatrues are capable of flying as well as birds; and if any should attempt it, that would be the best pattern for imitation.

After this, he might try what may be effected by the force of springs in lesser models, answerable unto *Archytas* his Dove, and *Regiomontanus* his Eagle; in which he must be careful to observe the various proportions betwixt the strength of the spring, the heaviness of the body, the breadth of the wings, the swiftness of the motion, &c.

From these he may by degrees ascend to some larger essays. CAP.

CAP. IX.

Of a perpetual motion. The seeming facility and real difficulty of any such contrivance. The several ways whereby it hath been atttempted, particularly by Chymistry.

IT is the chief inconvenience of all the *Automata* before mentioned, that they need a frequent repair of new strength; the causes whence their motion does proceed, being subject to fail and come to a period; and therefore it would be worth an enquiry, to examine, whether or no there may be made any such artificial contrivance, which might have the principle of moving from it self; so that the present motion should constantly be the cause of that which succeeds.

This is that great Secret in *Art*, which like the Philosopher's Stone in *Nature*, hath been the business and study of many more refined Wits, for divers ages together; and it may well be questioned, whether either
of

of them as yet, hath ever been found out, though if this have, yet like the other, it is not plainly treated of by any Author.

Not but that there are sundry discourses concerning this subject, but they are rather *conjectures* than *experiments*. And though many inventions in this kind, may at first view bear a great shew of probability; yet they will fail, being brought to trial, and will not answer in practise what they promised in speculation. Any one who hath been versed in these experiments must needs acknowledge that he hath been often deceived in his strongest confidence; when the imagination hath contrived the whole frame of such an instrument, and conceives that the event must fallibly answer its hopes; yet then does it strangely deceive in the proof, and discovers to us some defect, which we did not before take notice of.

Hence it is, that you will scarce talk with any one who hath never so little smattering in these arts, but he will instantly promise such a motion, as being but an easie atchievement, till further trial and experience hath taught him the difficulty of it. There being no enquiry that does more entice with the *probability*, and deceive with the *subtilty*. What one speaks wittily concerning the Philosophers Stone, may be justly applied to this, that it is *Casta meretrix*, a chast Whore, *Quia multos invitat, neminem admittit*, because it allures many, but admits none.

I shall briefly recite the several ways whereby this hath been attempted, or seems most likely to be effected, thereby to contract and facilitate the enquiries of those who are addicted to these kind of experiments; for when they know the defects of other inventions, they may the more easily avoid the same, or the like, in their own.

The ways whereby this hath been attempted, may be generally reduced to these three kinds:

1. By Chymical extractions.

2. By

Cap. 9. *Mechanical Motions.*

2. By Magnetical virtues.

3. By the natural affection of gravity.

1. The discovery of this hath been attempted by Chymistry. *Paracelsus* and his followers have bragged, that by their seperations and extractions, they can make a little world which shall have the same perpetual motions with this *Microcosme*, with the representation of all Meteors, Thunder, Snow, Rain, the courses of the sea in its ebbs and flows, and the like; But these miraculous promises would require as great a faith to believe them, as a power to perform them: And though they often talk of such great matters,

At nusquam totos inter qui talia cu-
  rant,
Apparet ullus, qui re miracula tanta
  Comprobet —

yet we can never see them confirmed by any real experiment; and then besides, every particular Author in that art, hath such a distinct language of his own, (all of them being so full

228 *Dædalus; or,* Lib. II.

of allegories and affected obscurities) that 'tis very hard for any one (unless he be throughly versed amongst them) to find out what they mean, much more to try it.

Eeten Mathem Recreat. Prob. 118.

One of these ways (as I find it set down) is this. Mix five ounces of ☿, with an equal weight of ♃ grind them together with ten ounces of sublimate, dissolve them in a Cellar upon some marble for the space of four days, till they become like oyl-olive; distil this with fire of chaff, or driving fire, and it will sublime into a dry substance: and so by repeating of these dissolvings and distillings, there will be at length produced divers small atomes, which being put into a glass well luted, and kept dry, will have a perpetual motion.

I cannot say any thing from experience against this; but methinks it does not seem very probable, because things that are forced up to such a vigorousness and activity, as these ingredients seem to be by their frequent

Cap. 9. Mechanical Motions. 229

quent sublimatings and distillings, are not likely to be of any duration; the more any thing is stretched beyond its usual nature, the less does it last, violence and perpetuity being no companions. And then besides, suppose it true, yet such a motion could not well be applied to any use, which must needs take much from the delight of it.

Amongst the Chymical experiments to this purpose, may be reckoned up that famous motion invented by *Cornelius Dreble*, and made for King *James*; wherein was represented the constant revolutions of the Sun and Moon, and that without the help either of spring or weights. *Marcellus Vranckhein*, speaking of the means whereby it was performed, he calls it, *Scintillula animæ magneticæ mundi, seu Astralis & insensibilis spiritus*; being that grand secret, for the discovery of which, those Dictators of Philosophy, *Democritus, Pythagoras, Plato*, did travel unto the Gymnosophists, and *Indian* Priests.

Celebrated in an Epigram by Hugo Grotius Hugo Epit. ad Ernest. and Lantg.

Q 3 The

The Author himself in his discourse upon it, does not at all reveal the way, how it was performed. But there is one *Thomas Tymme*, who was a familiar acquaintance of his, and did often pry into his works, (as he professes himself) who affirms it to be done thus; *By extractnig a fiery spirit out of the Mineral matter, joyning the same with his proper air, which included in the Axle-tree* (of the first moving wheel) *being hollow, carrieth the other wheels, making a continual rotation, except issue or vent be given in this hollow axle-tree, whereby the imprisoned spirit may get forth.*

What strange things may be done by such extractions, I know not, and therefore dare not condemn this relation as impossible; but methinks it sounds rather like a chymical dream, than a Philosophical truth. It seems this imprisoned spirit is now set at liberty, or else is grown weary, for the instrument (as I have heard) hath stood still for many years. It is here considerable, that any force is weakest near

Epist. ad Jacobum, Regem.

Philosophical dialogue. Confer. 2. cap. 4.

Cap.9. *Mechanical Motions.*

near the center of a wheel; and therefore though such a spirit might of it self have an agitation, yet it's not easily conceivable how it should have strength enough to carry the wheels about with it. And then the absurdity of the Author's citing this, would make one mistrust his mistake; he urges it as a strong argument against *Copernicus*, as if because *Dreble* did thus contrive in an Engine, the revolution of the heavens, and the immovableness of the earth, therefore it must needs follow, that 'tis the heavens which are moved, and not the earth. If his relation were no truer than his consequence, it had not been worth the citing.

CAP. X.

Of subterraneous lamps: divers historical relations concerning their duration for many hundred years together.

UNto this kind of Chymical experiments, we may most probably reduce those perpetual lamps, which for many hundred years together have continued burning without any new supply in the sepulchres of the Ancients, and might (for ought we know) have remained so for ever. All fire, and especially flame, being of an active and stirring nature, it cannot therefore subsist without motion; whence it may seem, that this great enquiry hath been this way accomplished: And therefore it will be worth our examination to search further into the particulars that concern this experiment. Though it be not so proper to the chief purpose of this discourse, which concerns *Mechanical Geometry*; yet the subtilty

and

and curiosity of it, may abundantly requite the impertinency.

There are sundry Authors who treat of this Subjection by the by, and in some particular passages, but none that I know of (except *Fortunius Licetus*) that hath writ purposely any set and large discourse concerning it: out of whom I shall borrow many of those relations and opinions, which may most naturally conduce to the present enquiry.

Lib. de reconditis antiquorum Lucernis.

For our fuller understanding of this, there are these particulars to be explained:

1. ὅτι, or *quod sit.*
2. διότι { *cur sit.* / *quomodo sit.* }

1. First then, for the ὅτι, or that there have been such lamps, it may be evident from sundry plain and undeniable testimonies: Saint *Austin* mentions one of them in a Temple dedicated to *Venus*, which was always exposed to the open weather, and could never be consumed or extinguished. To him assents the judicious

De Civit. Dei. l. 21. cap. 6.

Dedeperd. Tit. 35. De operibus Dei part 1. l. 4. c. 12.

cious *Zanchy*. *Pancyrollus* mentions a Lamp found in his time, in the sepulcher of *Tullia*, *Cicero*'s daughter, which had continued there for about 1550 years, but was presently extinguished upon the admission of new air. And 'tis commonly related of *Cedrenus*, that in *Justinian*'s time there was another burning lamp found in an old wall at * *Edessa*, which had remained so for above 500 years, there being a Crucifix placed by it, whence it should seem that they were in use also amongst some Christians.

* *Or Antioch. Licetus de Lucernis, l. 1. c. 7.*

But more especially remarkable is that relation celebrated by so many Authors, concerning *Olybius* his lamp, which had continued burning for 1500 years. The story is thus: As a rustick was digging the ground by *Padua*, he found an Urn or earthen pot, in which there was another Urn, and in this lesser, a lamp clearly burning; on each side of it there were two other Vessels, each of them full of a pure liquor, the one of gold, the other of Silver. *Ego Chymiæ artis, (si modo*

Cap. 10. Mechanical Motions.

modo vera potest esse ars Chymia) jurare ausim elementa & materiam omnium, (saith *Maturantius*, who had the possession of these things after they were taken up). On the bigger of these Urns there was this inscription:

Plutoni sacrum munus ne attingite fures.
  Ignotum est vobis hoc quod in orbe latet,
Namque elementa gravi clausit digesta labore.
  Vase sub hoc modico, Maximus Olybius.
Adsit fæcundo custos sibi copia cornu,
  Ne tanti pretium depereat laticis,

The lesser Urn was thus inscribed:
  Abite hinc pessimi fures,
  Vos quid vultis, vestris cum oculis emissitiis?
  Abite hinc vestro cum Mercurio
  Petasato Caduceatoque,
  Donum hoc Maximum, Maximus Olybius
  Plutoni sacrum facit.

Whence we may probably conjecture, that is was some Chymical secret,

cret, by which this was contrived.

Baptista Porta tells us of another lamp burning in an old marble sepulcher, belonging to some of the ancient *Romans*, inclosed in a glass vial, found in his time, about the year 1550, in the Isle *Nesis*, which had been buried there before our Saviour's coming.

Mag Natural. l. 12. c. ult.

In the Tomb of *Pallas* the *Arcadian* who was slain by *Turnus* in the *Trojan* war, there was found another burning lamp in the year of our Lord 1401. Whence it would seem that it had continued there for above two thousand and six hundred years: and being taken out, it did remain burning, notwithstanding either wind or water, with which some did strive to quench it; nor could it be extinguished till they had spilt the liquor in it.

Chron. Martin Fort. licet. de lucern. l. 1. c. 11.

Ludovicus Vives tells us of another lamp that did continue burning for 1050 years, which was found a little before his time.

Not. ad August. de Civit. Dei, l. 21. c. 6.

Such a lamp is likewise related to be

be seen in the sepulcher of *Francis Rosicross*, as is more largely expressed in the confession of that fraternity

There is another relation of a certain man, who upon occasion digging somewhat deep in the ground, did meet with something like a door, having a wall on each hand of it; from which having cleared the earth, he forced opon the door; upon this there was discovered a fair Vault, and towards the farther side of it, the statue of a man in Armour, sitting by a table, leaning upon his left arm, and holding a scepter in his right hand, with a lamp burning before him; the floor of this Vault being so contrived, that upon the first step into it, the statue would erect it self from its leaning posture, upon the second step it did lift up the scepter to strike, and before a man could approach near enough to take hold of the lamp, the statue did strike and break it to pieces. Such care was there taken that it might not be stoln away, or discovered.

Our learned *Cambden* in his description *pag. 572.*

tion of *Yorkshire*, speaking of the tomb of *Constantius Chlorus*, broken up in these later years, mentions such a lamp to be found within it.

There are sundry other relations to this purpose. *Quod ad lucernas attinet, illæ in omnibus fere monumentis inveniuntur,* (saith *Jutherius*). In most of the ancient Monuments there is some kind of lamp, (though of the ordinary sort): But those persons who were of greatest note and wisdom, did procure such as might last without supply, for so many ages together. *Pancirollus* tells us, that it was usual for the Nobles amongst the Romans, to take special care in their last wills, that they might have a lamp in their Monuments. And to this purpose they did usually give liberty unto some of their slaves on this condition, that they should be watchful in maintaining and preserving it. From all which relations, the first particular of this enquiry, concerning the being or existence of such lamps, may sufficiently appear.

De jure manium. l. 2. c. 32.

De perdit. Ti. 62.

CAP.

Cap. 11. *Mechanical Motions.* 239

CAP. XI.
Several opinions concerning the nature and reason of these perpetual Lamps.

THere are two opinions to be answered, which do utterly overthrow the chief consequence from these relations.

1. Some think that these lights so often discovered in the ancient tombs, were not fire or flame, but only some of those bright bodies which do usually shine in dark places.

2. Others grant them to be fire, but yet think them to be then first enkindled by the admission of new air when these sepulchres were opened.

1. There are divers bodies (saith *Aristotle*) which shine in the dark, as rotten wood, the scales of some fishes, stones, the glow-worm, the eyes of divers creatures. *Cardan* tells us of a bird in new *Spain*, called *Cocoyum*, whose whole body is very bright, but his eyes almost equal to the light of

De anima, l. 2. c. 7.

Subtil. l. 9.

a

a candle, by which alone in a dark night one may both write and read; By these the *Indians* (saith he) use to eat their feasting Suppers.

It is commonly related and believed, that a Carbuncle does shine in the dark like a burning coal, from whence it hath its * name. To which purpose there is a story in *Ælian*, of a Stork, that by a certain woman was cured of a broken thigh, in gratitude to whom, this fowl afterwards flying by her, did let fall into her lap a bright Carbuncle, which (saith he) would in the night time shine as clear as a lamp. But this and the like old relations are now generally disbelieved and rejected by learned men: *Doctissimorum omnium consensu, hujusmodi gemmæ non inveniuntur*, saith *Boetius de Boot*) a man very much skilled in, and inquisite after such matters; nor is there any one of name that does from his own eye-sight or experience affirm the real existence of any gem so qualified.

Some have thought that the light in

* *Carbo Pyropus Historia Animal. l.8*

De lapid & Gemmis. l. 2. c. 8.

Cap. 11. *Mechanical Motions.*

in ancient tombs hath been occasioned from some such bodies as these. For if there had been any possibility to preserve fire so long a space, 'tis likely then that the *Israelites* would have known the way, who were to keep it perpetually for their Sacrifices.

Vide Licet. de lucern. l. 2.

But to this opinion it might be replied, That none of these *Nocticula*, or night-shining bodies have been observed in any of the Ancient Sepulchres, and therefore this is a meer imaginary conjecture; and then besides, some of these lamps have been taken out burning, and continued so for a considerable space afterwards. As for the supposed conveniency of them, for the perpetuating of the holy fire amongst the Jews, it may as well be feared lest these should have occasioned their Idolatry, unto which that Nation was so strongly addicted upon every slight occasion; nor may it seem strange, if the providence of God should rather permit this fire sometimes to go out, that so by their earnest prayers, being a-

gain

their belief, concerning the souls immortality, after its departure out of the body, a lamp amongst the *Egyptians* being the *Hieroglyphick* of life. And therefore they that could not procure such lamps, were yet careful to have the image and representations of them ingraved on their Tombs.

Others conceive them to be by way of gratitude to those infernal Deities, who took the charge and custody of their dead bodies, *remaining* always with them in their Tombs, and were therefore called *Dii manes*.

Others are of opinion, that these lamps were only intended to make their sepulchres more pleasant and lightsome, that they might not seem to be imprisoned in a dismal and uncomfortable place. True indeed, the dead body cannot be sensible of the light, no more could it of its want of burial; yet the same instinct which did excite it to the desire of one, did also occasion the other.

Licetus concludes this ancient custome to have a double end: 1. Politick,

De Lucernis l.3.c.8.

litick, for the distinction of such as were nobly born, in whose Monuments only they were used. 2. *Natural*, to preserve the body and soul from darkness; for it was a common opinion amongst them, that the souls also were much conversant about those places where the bodies were buried.

CAP. XII.

The most probable conjecture how these lamps were framed.

THE greatest difficulty of this enquiry doth consist in this last particular, concerning the manner how or by what possible means any such perpetual flame may be contriv'd.

Quomodo fint.

For the discovery of which, there are two things to be more especially considered.

1. The snuff or wiek, which must administer unto the flame.

2. The oyl, which must nourish it.

For the firſt, it is generally granted that there are divers ſubſtances which will retain fire without conſuming: ſuch is that Mineral which they call the Salamanders-wool, ſaith our learned * *Bacon*. *Ipſe expertus ſum villos Salamandræ non conſumi*, ſaith † *Joachimus Fortius*; and * *Wecker* from his own knowledg affirms the ſame of *Plumeallum*, that being formed into the likeneſs of a wiek, will adminiſter to the flame, and yet not conſume it ſelf. Of this nature likewiſe was that which the Ancients did call *Linum vivum*, or *Asbeſtinum*: of this they were wont to make garments that were not deſtroyed, but purified by fire; and whereas the ſpots or foulneſs of other cloaths are waſhed out, in theſe they were uſually burnt away. The bodies of the ancient Kings were wrapped in ſuch garments when they were put in the funeral pile, that their aſhes might be therein preſerved, without the mixture of any other. The materials of them were not from any herb or vegetable,

Nat. Hiſt. exper. 774.
† *Lib. exper.*
* *De Secretis, l. 3. c. 2*

Or *Linum Carpaſium. Plutarch de Oracul. defectu.*

Plin. Hiſt. l. 19. c. 1.

Cap. 12. *Mechanical Motions.*

ble, as other textils, but from a stone called *Amiantus*, which being bruised by a hammar, and its earthy nature shaken out, retains certain hairy substances, which may be spun and woven as hemp or flax. *Pliny* says, that for the preciousness of it, it did almost equal the price of pearls. *Pancirollus* tells us, that it was very rare, and esteemed precious in ancient times; but now is scarce found or known in any place, and therefore he reckons it amongst the things that are lost. But *L. Vives* affirms, that he hath often seen wieks made of it at *Paris*, and the same matter woven into a napkin at *Lovaine*, which was cleansed by being burnt in the fire.

Deperd. Tit. 4.

In Aug. de Civ. D. Dei l. 2 l. c. 6.

'Tis probable from these various relations, that there was several sorts of it, some of a more precious, others of a baser kind, that was found in *Cyprus*, the deserts of *India*, and a certain Province of *Asia*: this being common in some parts of *Italy*, but is so short and brittle, that it cannot be spun into a thred. And therefore is useful only for the wieks of perpetual lamps, saith *Boetius de Boot*. Some of this, or very like it, I have upon enquiry lately procured and experimented. But whether it be the stone *Asbestus*, or only *Plume-allum*, I cannot certainly affirm. For it seems they are both so very like, as to be commonly sold for one another (saith the same Author). However, it does truly agree in this common quality ascribed unto both, of being incombustible, and not consumable by fire: But yet there is this inconvenience, that it doth contract so much fuliginous matter from the earthy parts of the oyl, (though is was tryed with some of the purest oyl, which is ordinary to be bought) that in a very few days it did choak and extinguish the flame. There may possibly be some Chymical way so to purifie and defecate this oyl, that it shall not spend into a sooty matter.

However if the liquor be of a close and glutinous consistency, it may burn without any snuff, as we see

De Lapid. & gemmis. l. 2. c. 204.

Cap. 12. *Mechanical Motions.*

in Camphire, and some other bituminous substances. And it is probable that most of the ancient lamps were of this kind, because the exactest relations (to my remembrance) do not mention any that have been found with such wieks.

But herein will consist the greatest difficulty, to find out what invention there might be for their duration. Concerning which there are sundry opinions.

Saint *Austin* speaking of that Lamp in one of the Heathen Temples, thinks that it might either be done by Magick, the Devil thinking thereby to promote the worship and esteem of that Idol to which it was dedicated; or else that the art of man might make it of some such material, as the stone *Asbestus*, which being once enkindled, will burn without being consumed. As others (saith he) have contrived as great a wonder in appearance, from the natural virtue of another stone, making an iron-image seem to hang in the air, by rea-

De Civ. Dei l. 21 c. 6.

Zanch. de Operibus Dei, par. 1 l. 4. c. 12.

reason of two load-stones, the one being placed in the Ceiling, the other in the floor.

Others are of opinion, that this may be effected in a hollow vessel, exactly luted or stopped up in all the vents of it. And then, if a lamp be supposed to burn in it, but for the least moment of time, it must continue so always, or else there would be a *Vacuum*, which nature is not capable of; If you ask how it shall be nourished? it is answered, that the oyl of it being turned into smoak and vapours, will again be converted into its former nature; for otherwise, if it should remain rarefied in so thin a substance, then there would not be room enough for that fume which must succeed it; and so on the other side, there might be some danger of the *Penetration* of bodies, which nature doth as much abhor. To prevent both which, as it is in the Chymical circulations, where the same body is oftentimes turned from liquor into vapour, and from vapour into liquor again; so

Cap. 12. *Mechanical Motions.*

in this experiment, the same oyl shall be turned into fume, and that fume shall again convert into oyl. Always provided, that this oyl which nourishes the lamp, be supposed of so close and tenacious a substance, that may slowly evaporate, and so there will be the more leisure for nature to perfect these circulations. According to which contrivance, the lamp within this vessel can never fail, being always supplied with sufficient nourishment. That which was found in the Isle *Nesis*, inclosed in a glass vial, mentioned by *Baptista Porta*, is thought to be made after some such manner as this.

Others conceive it possible to extract such an oyl out of some Minerals, which shall for a long space serve to nourish the flame of a lamp with very little or no expence of its own substance. To which purpose (say they) if gold be dissolved into an unctuous humour; or if the radical moisture of that metal were separated, it might be contrived to burn

(perhaps

Wolphang Lazius, l. 3. c. 18. Camb. Brit. p. 572.

(perhaps for ever, or at least) for many ages together, without being consumed. For if gold it self (as experience shews) be so untameable by the fire, that after many meltings, and violent heats, it does scarce diminish; 'tis probable then, that being dissolved into an oylie substance, it might for many hundred years together continue burning.

There is a little Chymical discourse, to prove that *Urim* and *Thummim* is to be made by art; the Author of this Treatise affirms that place, *Gen.* 6. 16. where God tells *Noah*, *A window shalt thou make in the Ark*, to be very unfitly rendered in our Translation a window, because the Original word צהר signifies properly splendor or light; and then besides, the air being at that time so extremely darkned with the clouds of that excessive rain, a window could be but of very little use in regard of light, unless there were some other help for it; from whence he conjectures that both this splendor, and so likewise the Urim

and

Cap. 12. Mechanical Motions. 253

and Thummim, were artificial Chymical preparations of light, answerable to these subterraneous lamps; or in his own phrase, it hath *the universal spirit fixed in a transparant body.*

It is the opinion of *Licetus* (who hath more exactly searched into the subtilties of this enquiry) that fire does not need any humour for the nourishment of it, but only to detain it from flying upwards. For being it self one of the chief elements (saith he out of *Theophrastus*) it were absurd to think that it could not subsist without something to feed it. As for that substance which is consumed by it, this cannot be said to foment or preserve the same fire, but only to generate new. For the better understanding of this, we must observe, that there may be a threefold proportion betwixt fire, and the humour or matter of it. Either the humour does exceed the strength of the fire, or the fire does exceed the humour; and according to both these, the flame doth presently vanish. Or else

De Lucernis, c. 20, 21.

else lastly, they may be both equal in their virtues, (as it is betwixt the radical moisture and natural heat in living creatures) and then neither of them can overcome or destroy the other.

Those ancient lamps of such long duration, were of this later kind. But now, because the qualities of heat or cold, dryness or moisture in the ambient air, may alter this equality of proportion betwixt them, and make one stronger than the other; therefore to prevent this, the Ancients did hide these lamps in some caverns of the earth, or close monuments: And hence is it, that at the opening of these, the admission of new air unto the lamp does usually cause so great an inequality betwixt the flame and the oyl, that it is presently extinguished.

But still the greatest difficulty remains how to make any such exact proportion betwixt an unctuous humour, and such an active quality, as the heat of fire; or this equality being

Cap. 12. *Mechanical Motions.*

ing made, it is yet a further difficulty how it may be preserved. To which purpose, *Licetus* thinks it possible to extract an inflameable oyl from the stone *Asbestus*, *Amiantus*, or the metal Gold, which being of the same pure and homogenious nature with those bodies, shall be so proportioned unto the heat of fire, that it cannot be consumed by it, but being once inflamed should continue for many ages, without any sensible diminution.

If it be in the power of Chymistry to perform such strange effects as are commonly experimented in that which they call *aurum fulminans*, one scruple of which shall give a louder blow, and be of greater force in descent, than half a pound of ordinary Gunpowder in ascent; why may it not be as feasible by the same art to extract such an oyl as is here enquired after: since it must needs be more difficult to make a fire which of its own inclination shall tend downwards, than to contrive such an unctuous

ctuous liquor, wherein fire shall be maintained for many years without any new supply?

Thus have I briefly set down the relations and opinions of divers learned men concerning these perpetual lamps; of which, though there have been so many sundry kinds, and several ways to make them, (some being able to resist any violence of weathers, others being easily extinguished by any little alteration of the air; some being inclosed round about within glass, others being open); yet now they are all of them utterly perished amongst the other ruines of time; and those who are most versed in the search after them, have only recovered such dark conjectures, from which a man cannot clearly reduce any evident principle that may encourage him to a particular trial.

CAP. XIII.

Concerning several attempts of contriving a perpetual motion by Magnetical virtues.

THE second way whereby the making of a perpetual motion hath been attempted, is by Magnetical virtues; which are not without some strong probabilities of proving effectual to this purpose: especially when we consider, that the heavenly revolutions, (being as the first pattern imitated and aimed at in these attempts) are all of them performed by the help of these qualities. This great Orb of earth, and all the other Planets being but as so many Magnetical Globes endowed with such various and continual motions, as may be most agreable to the purposes for which they were intended. And therefore most of the Authors who treat concerning this invention, do agree, that the likeliest way to effect it, is by these kind of qualities.

S It

It was the opinion of *Pet. Peregrinus*, and there is an example pretended for it in *Bettinus*) *Apiar.* 9. *Progym.* 5. *pro.* 11). That a Magnetical Globe or Terella, being rightly placed upon its poles, would of it self have a constant rotation, like the diurnal motion of the earth. But this is commonly exploded, as being against all experience.

Others think it possible, so to contrive several pieces of steel, and a loadstone, that by their continual attraction and expulsion of one another, they may cause a perpetual revolution of a wheel; Of this opinion were [a] *Taisner*, [b] *Pet. Peregrinus*, and [c] *Cardan*, out of *Antonius de Fantis*. But D. *Gilbert*, who was more especially versed in Magnetical experiments, concludes it to be a vain and groundless fancy.

But amongst all these kind of inventions, that is most likely, wherein a loadstone is so disposed, that it shall draw unto it on a reclined plane, a bullet of steel; which steel, as it ascends

Gilbert. de Magnet. Cabœus Philos. Magnet. l. 4. c. 20.

Athanas. Kircher. de Arte Magnes. l. 1. par. 2. prop. 13. p. 4.

[a] *Tract. de motu continuo.*
[b] *De Rota perpetui motus. par. 2. c. 3.*
[c] *De variet. rerum l. 9. c. 48. De magnet. l. 2. c. 35.*

Cap. 13. *Mechanical Motions.* 259

scends near to the loadstone, may be contrived to fall down through some hole in the plane, and so to return unto the place from whence at first it began to move; and being there, the loadstone will again attract it upwards, till coming to this hole, it will fall down again: and so the motion will be perpetual, as may be more easily conceivable by this figure.

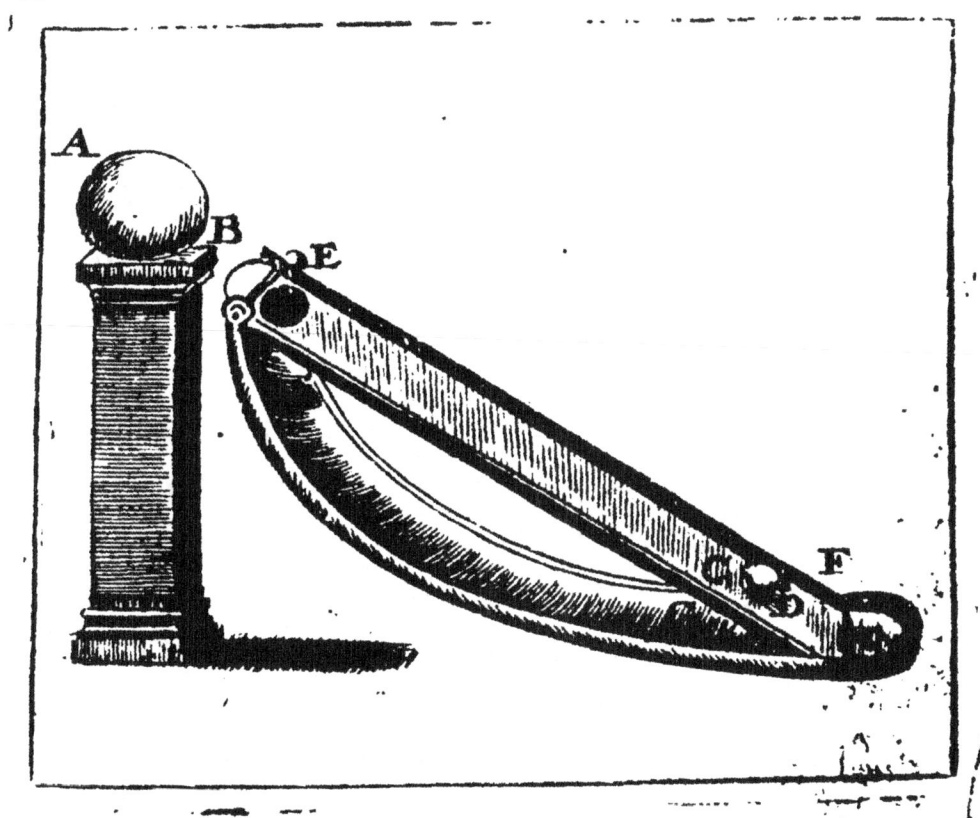

Suppose

Suppose the loadstone to be represented at *A B*, which though it have not strength enough to attract the bullet *C*, directly from the ground, yet may do it by the help of the plane *E F*. Now when the bullet is come to the top of this plane, its own gravity (which is supposed to exceed the strength of the loadstone) will make it fall into that hole at *E*: and the force it receives in this fall, will carry it with such a violence unto the other end of this arch, that it will open the passage which is there made for it, and by its return will again shut it; so that the bullet (as at the first) is in the same place whence it was attracted, and consequently must move perpetually.

But however this invention may seem to be of such strong probability, yet there are sundry particulars which may prove it insufficient. For,

1. This bullet of steel must first be touched and have its several poles, or else there can be little or no attraction of it. Suppose *C* in the steel

to

to be anſwerable unto *A* in the ſtone, and to *B*; In the attraction, *C D* muſt always be directed anſwerable to *A B*, and ſo the motion will be more difficult, by reaſon there can be no rotation or turning round of the bullet, but it muſt ſlide up with the line *C D*, anſwerable to the axis *A B*.

2. In its fall from *E* to *G*, which is *motus elementaris*, and proceeds from its gravity, there muſt needs be a rotation of it, and ſo 'tis odds but it happens wrong in the riſe, the poles in the bullet being not in the ſame direction to thoſe in the magnet; and if in this reflux it ſhould ſo fall out, that *D* ſhould be directed towards *B*, there ſhould be rather a flight than an attraction, ſince thoſe two ends do *repell* and not draw one another.

3 If the loadſtone *A B*, have ſo much ſtrength that it can attract the bullet in *F*, when it is not turned round, but does only ſlide upon the plane, whereas its own gravity would roul it downwards: then it is evident,

the

the sphere of this activity and strength would be so increased when it approaches much nearer, that it would not need the assistance of the plane, but would draw it immediately to it self without that help, and so the bullet would not fall down through the hole, but ascend to the stone, and consequently cease its motion. For if the loadstone be of force enough to draw the bullet on the plane, at the distance *F B*, then must the strength of it be sufficient to attract it immediately unto it self, when it is so much nearer as *E B*. And if the gravity of the bullet be supposed so much to exceed the strength of the Magnet, that it cannot draw it directly when it is so near, then will it not be able to attract the bullet up the plane, when it is so much further off.

So that none of all these Magnetical experiments, which have been as yet discovered, are sufficient for the effecting of a perpetual motion, though these kind of qualities seem most conducible unto it, and perhaps

Cap. 14. *Mechanical Motions.*

haps hereafter it may be contrived from them.

CAP. XIV.
The seeming probability of effecting a continual motion by solid weights in a hollow wheel or sphere.

THE third way whereby the making a perpetual motion hath been attempted, is by the natural affection of gravity; when the heaviness of several bodies is so contrived, that the same motion which they give in their descent, may be able to carry them up again.

But amongst the possibility of any such invention, it is thus objected by *Cardan*; All sublunary bodies have a direct motion either of ascent or descent; which, because it does refer to some term, therefore cannot be perpetual, but must needs cease when it is arrived at the place unto which it naturally tends.

I answer, Though this may prove

*Subtil.l.17
De Var.
Rerum l.
9.c.48.*

that

that there is no natural motion of any particular heavy body, which is perpetual; yet it doth not hinder but that it is poffible from them to contrive fuch an artificial revolution as fhall conftantly be the caufe of it felf.

Thofe bodies which may be ferviceable to this purpofe, are diftinguifhable into two kinds.

1. Solid and confiftent, as weights of metal or the like.

2. Fluid or fliding, as water, fand, &c.

D. Flud. Tract. 2. part 7. l. 2. c. 4. & 7.

Both thefe ways have been attempted by many, though with very little or no fuccefs. Other mens conjectures in this kind you may fee fet down by divers Authors. It would be too tedious to repeat them over, or fet forth their draughts. I fhall only mention two new ones, which (if I am not over partial) feem altogether as probable as any of thefe kinds that have been yet invented; and till experience had difcovered their defect and infufficiency, I did certainly

Cap. 14. Mechanical Motions. 265

tainly conclude them to be infallible.

The first of these contrivances was by solid weights being placed in some hollow wheel or sphere, unto which they should give a perpetual revolution. For (as the Philosopher hath largely proved) only a circular motion can properly be perpetual.

Arist. Phis. l. 8. c. 12.

But for the better conceiving of this invention, it is requisite that we rightly understand some principles in *Trochilicks*, or the Art of Wheel-instruments: As chiefly, the relation betwixt the parts of a wheel, and those of a Ballance; the several proportions in the Semidiameter of a wheel being answerable to the sides in a Ballance, where the weight is multiplied according to its distance from the center.

Arist. Mechan. c. 2. De ratione libræ ad circulum.

Thus

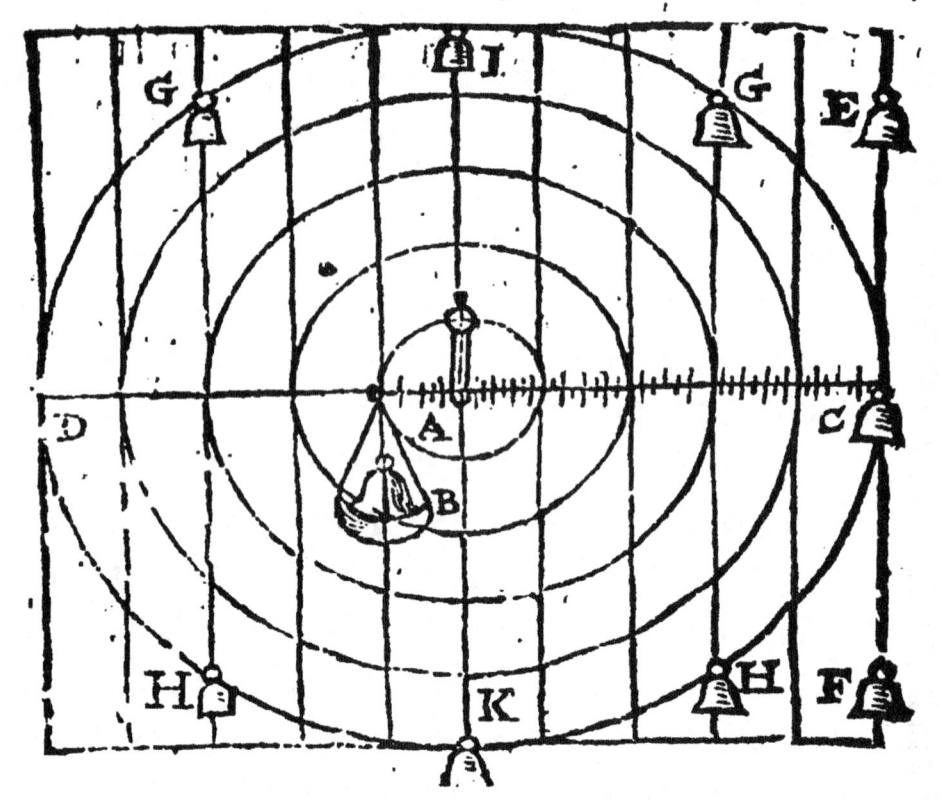

Thus suppose the center to be at *A*, and the Diameter of the wheel *DC*, to be divided into equal parts (as is here expressed) it is evident according to the former ground, that one pound at *C*, will be equiponderate to five pound at *B*, because there is such a proportion betwixt their several distances from the Center. And it is not material whether or no these several weights be placed horizontally; for though *B* do hang lower than

Cap. 14. Mechanical Motions. 267

than C, yet this does not at all concern the heaviness; or though the plummet C were placed much higher than it is at E, or lower at F, yet would it still retain the same weight which it had at C, because the plummets (as is the nature of all heavy bodies) do tend downwards by a straight line: So that their several gravities are to be measured by that part of the horizontal Semidiameter which is directly either below or above them. Thus when the plummet C, shall be moved either to G or H, it will lose $\frac{2}{3}$ of its former heaviness, and be equally ponderous as if it were placed in the ballance at the number 3; and if we suppose it to be situated at I or K, then the weight of it will lie wholly upon the Center, and not at all conduce to the motion of the wheel on either side. So that the straight lines which pass through the divisions of the diameter, may serve to measure the heaviness of any weight in its several situations.

These things throughly considered,

it

it seems very possible and easie for a man to contrive the plummets of a wheel, that they may be always heavier in their fall, than in their ascent, and so consequently that they should give a perpetual motion to the wheel it self: Since it is impossible for that to remain unmoved, as long as one side in it is heavier than the other.

For the performance of this, the weights must be so ordered, 1. That in their descent they may fall from the Center, and in their ascent may rise nearer to it. 2. That the fall of each plummet may begin the motion of that which should succeed it. As in this following Diagram.

Where

Cap. 14. *Mechanical Motions.* 269

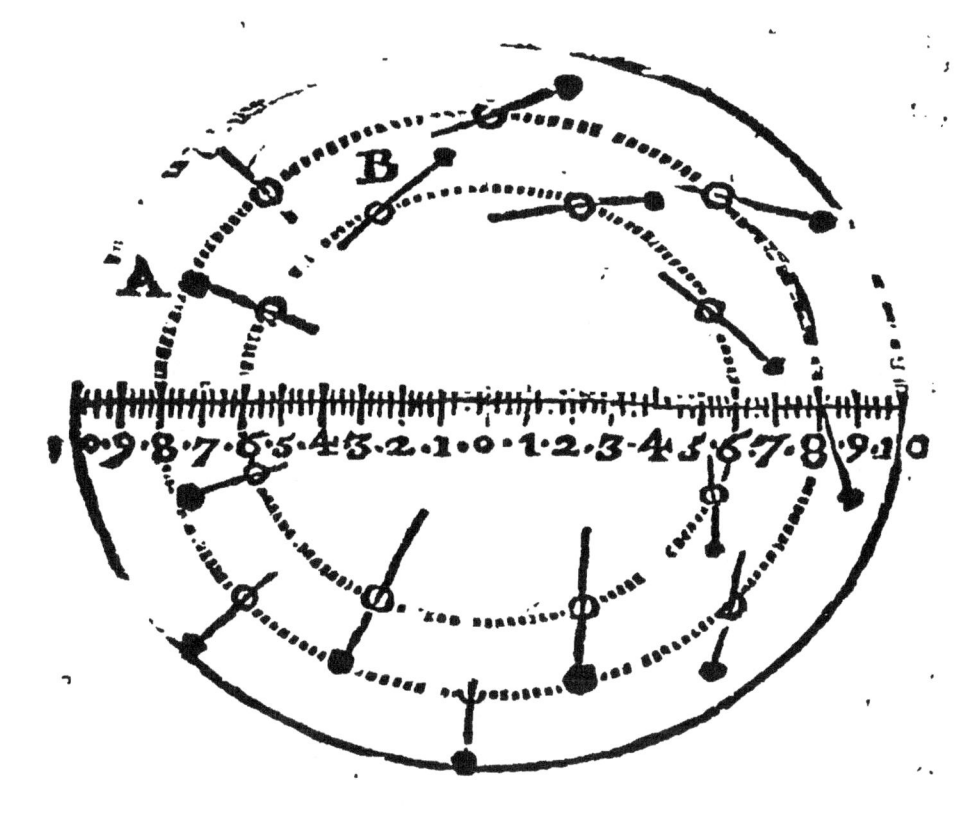

Where there are 16 plummets, 8 in the inward circle, and as many in the outward, (the equality being to arise from their situation, it is therefore most convenient that the number of them be even). The eight inward plummets are supposed to be in themselves so much heavier than the other, that in the wheel they may be of equal weight with these above them, and then the fall of these will be of sufficient force to bring down

down the other. For example, if the outward be each of them 4 ounces, then the inward muſt be 5, becauſe the outward is diſtant from the center 5 of thoſe parts, whereof the inward is but 4. Each pair of theſe weights ſhould be joyned together by a little ſtring or chain, which muſt be faſtned about the middle betwixt the bullet and the center of that plummet, which is to fall firſt, and at the top of the other.

When theſe bullets in their deſcent are at their fartheſt diſtance from the center of the wheel, then ſhall they be ſtopped, and reſt on the pins placed to that purpoſe; and ſo in their riſing there muſt be other pins to keep them in a convenient poſture and diſtance from the center, leſt approaching too near unto it, they thereby become unfit to fall, when they ſhall come to the top of the deſcending ſide.

This may be otherwiſe contrived with ſome different circumſtances; but they will all redound to the ſame effect.

Cap. 14. Mechanical Motions. 271

effect. By such an engine it seems very probable, that a man may produce a perpetual motion. The distance of the plummets from the center increasing their weight on one side; and their being tyed to one another, causing a constant succession in their falling.

But now, upon experience I have found this to be fallacious; and the reason may sufficiently appear by a calculation of the heaviness of each plummet, according to its several scituations; which may easily be done by those perpendiculars that cut the diameter, (as was before explained, and is here expressed in five of the plummets on the descending side). From such a calculation it will be evident, that both the sides of this wheel will equiponderate, and so consequently that the supposed inequality, whence the motion should proceed, is but imaginary and groundless. On the descending side, the heaviness of each plummet may be measured according to these numbers, (supposing the diameter

ameter of the wheel to be divided into twenty parts, and each of those subdivided into four).

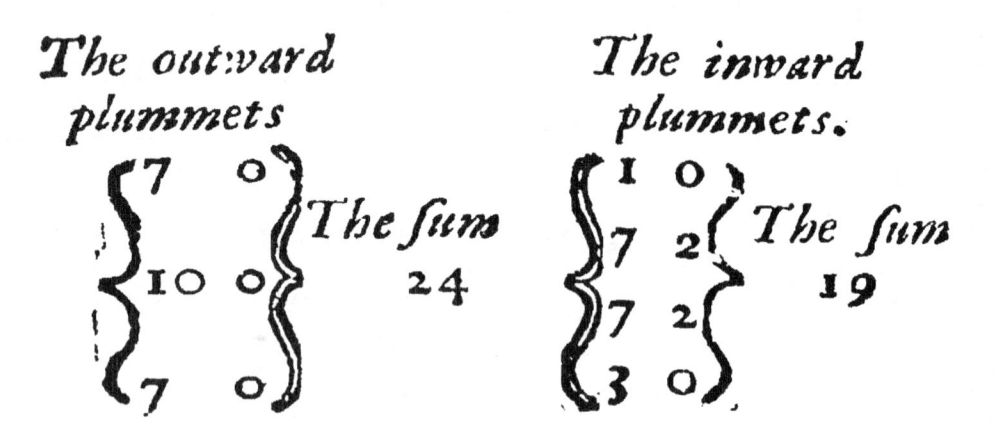

The outward plummets
$$\begin{Bmatrix} 7 & 0 \\ 10 & 0 \\ 7 & 0 \end{Bmatrix} \text{The sum } 24$$

The inward plummets.
$$\begin{Bmatrix} 1 & 0 \\ 7 & 2 \\ 7 & 2 \\ 3 & 0 \end{Bmatrix} \text{The sum } 19$$

On the ascending side the weights are to be reckoned according to these degrees,

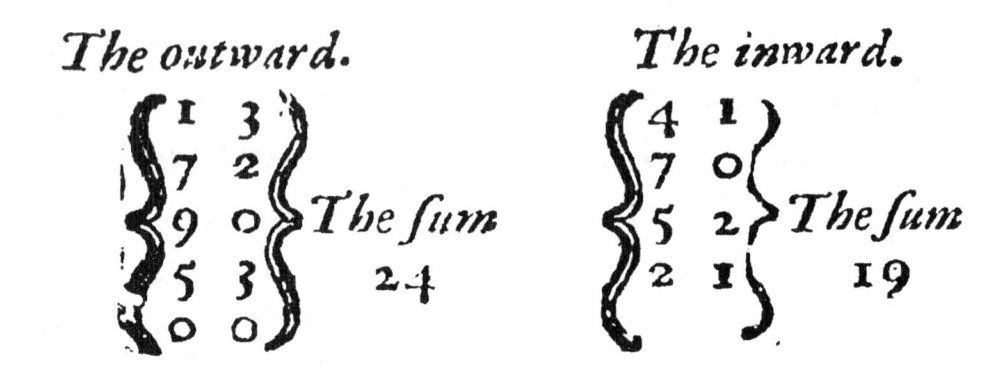

The outward.
$$\begin{Bmatrix} 1 & 3 \\ 7 & 2 \\ 9 & 0 \\ 5 & 3 \\ 0 & 0 \end{Bmatrix} \text{The sum } 24$$

The inward.
$$\begin{Bmatrix} 4 & 1 \\ 7 & 0 \\ 5 & 2 \\ 2 & 1 \end{Bmatrix} \text{The sum } 19$$

The sum of which last numbers is equal with the former, and therefore both the sides of such a wheel, in this situation will equiponderate.

If

Cap. 14. *Mechanical Motions.*

If it be objected, That the plummet *A* should be contrived to pull down the other at *B*, and then the descending side will be heavier than the other.

For answer to this, it is considerable,

1. That these bullets towards the top of the wheel, cannot descend till they come to a certain kind of inclination.

2. That any lower bullet hanging upon the other above it, to pull it down, must be conceived, as if the weight of it were in that point where its string touches the upper; at which point this bullet will be of less heaviness in respect of the wheel, than if it did rest in its own place: So that both the sides of it in any kind of situation may equipondeate.

T CAP.

CAP. XV.

Of composing a perpetual motion by fluid weights. Concerning Archimedes *his water-screw. The great probability of accomplishing this enquiry by the help of that; with the fallibleness of it upon experiment.*

That which I shall mention as the last way, for the trial of this experiment, is by contriving it in some water-instrument; which may seem altogether as probable and easie as any of the rest, because that element by reason of its fluid and subtil nature (whereby of its own accord it searches out the lower and more narrow passages) may be most pliable to the mind of the Artificer. Now the usual means for the ascent of water, is either by *Suckers* or *Forcers*, or something equivalent thereunto; Neither of which may be conveniently applied unto such a work as this, because there is required unto each of them so much or more strength, as may be answerable

Cap. 15. Mechanical Motions.

ble to the full weight of the water that is to be drawn up; and then besides, they move for the most part by fits and snatches, so that it is not easily conceivable, how they should conduce unto such a motion, which by reason of its perpetuity must be regular and equal.

But amongst all other ways to this purpose, that invention of *Archimedes* is incomparably the best, which is usually called *Cochlea*, or the *Water-screw*, being framed by the Helical revolution of a cavity about the Cylinder. We have not any discourse from the Author himself concerning it, nor is it certain whether he ever writ any thing to this purpose. But if he did, yet as the injury of time hath deprived us of many other his excellent works, so likewise of this, amongst the rest.

Athenæus speaking of that great ship built by *Hiero*, in the framing of which there were 300 Carpenters employed for a year together, besides many other hirelings for carriages,

Dipnosop. l. 5.

and such servile works, mentions this instrument, as being instead of a pump for that vast ship; by t' help of which, one man might easily and speedily drain out the water, though it were very deep.

Diodorus Siculus speaking of this engine, tells us, that *Archimedes* invented it when he was in *Egypt*, and that it was used in that Country for the draining those pits and lower grounds, whence the waters of *Nilus* could not return. Φιλοτέχνε δ' ὄντ@ τῷ ὀργάνῳ καθ' ὑπερβολὴν, (saith the same Author). It being an engine so ingenious and artificial, as cannot be sufficiently expressed or commended. And so (it should seem) the Smith in *Millain* conceived it to be, who having without any teaching or information found it out, and therefore thinking himself to be the first inventor, fell mad with the meer joy of it.

The nature and manner of making this, is more largely handled by *Vitruvius*.

Biblioth. l. 1.

Cardan. Subt. l. 1. De sapient. l. 5.

Architect. l. 10. c. 11.

The

Cap. 15. *Mechanical Motions.*

The Figure of it is after this manner,

Where you see there is a Cylinder *A A*, and a spiral cavity or pipe twining about it, according to equal revolutions *B B*. The axis and centers of its motions are at the points *C D*, upon which being turned, it will so happen that the same part of the pipe which was now lowermost, will presently become higher, so that the water does ascend by descending; ascending in comparison to the whole instrument, and descending in respect of its several parts. This being one of the strangest wonders amongst those many, wherein these Mathematical arts do abound, that a heavy body should rise by falling down; and the farther it passes by its own natural motion of descent, by so much higher still shall it ascend; which though it seem so evidently to contradict all reason and Philosophy; yet in this instrument it may be manifested both by demonstration and sense.

This pipe or cavity for the matter of it, cannot easily be made of metal, by reason of its often turnings; but for trial, there might be such a cavity, cut in a column of wood, and afterwards covered over with tin plate.

For the form and manner of making this screw, *Vitruvius* does prescribe these two rules:

1. That there must be an equality observed betwixt the breadth of the pipe, and the distance of its several circumvolutions.

2. That there must be such a proportion

Cap. 15. *Mechanical Motions.*

portion betwixt the length of the instrument, and its elevation, as is answerable to the *Pythagorical Trigon*. If the Hypotenusal, or Screw be 5, the perpendicular or elevation must be 3, and the basis 4.

David Rivalt. Com. in Archim. opera. externa.

However (with his leave) neither of these proportions are generally necessary, but should be varied according to other circumstances. As for the breadth of the pipe in respect of its revolutions, it is left at liberty, and may be contrived according to the quantity of water which it should contain. The chief thing to be considered is the obliquity or closeness of these circumvolutions. For the nearer they are unto one another, the higher may the instrument be erected; there being no other guide for its true elevation but this.

And because the right understanding of this particular is one of the principal matters that concern the use of this engine, therefore I shall endeavour with brevity and perspicuity to explain it. The first thing to be inquired after, is what kind of inclination these Helical revolutions of the Cylinder have unto the Horizon; which may be thus found out.

Let AB represent a Cylinder with two perfect revolutions in it; unto which Cylinder the perpendicular line CD is equal: the basis DE being supposed to be double unto the compass or circumference of the Cylinder. Now it is certain that the angle CED, is the same with that by which the revolutions on the Cylinder are framed; and that the line EC, in comparison to the basis ED, does shew the inclination of these revolutions unto the Horizon. The ground and demonstration of this, are more fully set down by *Guidus Ubaldus*, in his Mechanicks, and that other

Cap. 15. *Mechanical Motions.* 281

other Treatise *De Cochlea*, which he writ purposely for the explication of this instrument, where the subtilties of it are largely and excellently handled.

Now if this Screw which was before perpendicular, be supposed to decline unto the Horizon by the angle *F B G*, as in this second Figure;

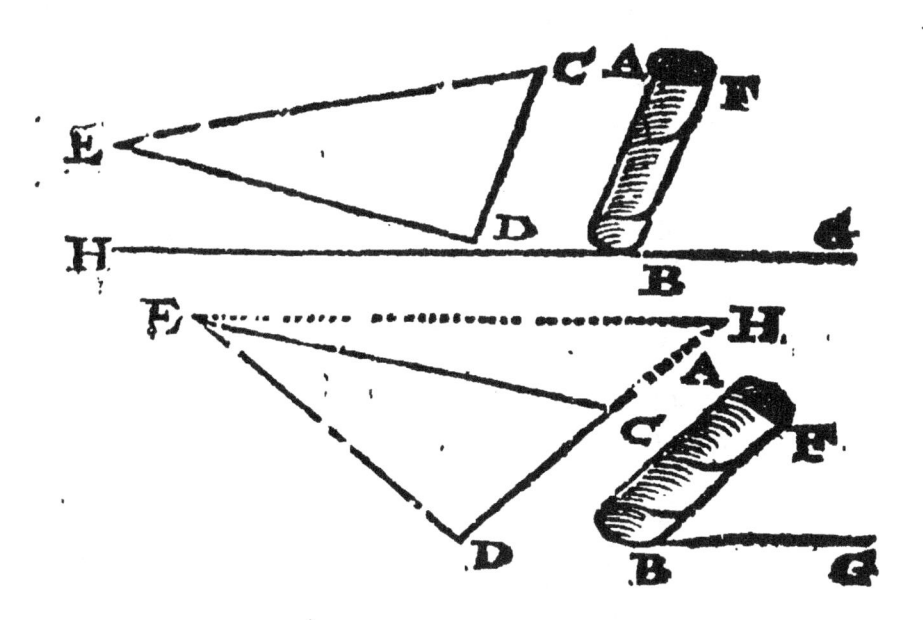

then the inclination of the revolutions in it, will be increased by the angle *E D H*, though these revolutions will still remain in a kind of ascent, so that water cannot be turned through them.

But

But now if the Screw be placed so far declining, that the angle of its inclination *F B G*, be less than the angle *E C D*, in the triangle, as in this other Diagram under the former; then the revolutions of it will descend to the Horizon, as does the line *E C*, and in such a posture, if the Screw be turned round, water will ascend through its cavity. Whence it is easie to conceive the certain declination wherein any Screw must be placed for its own conveyance of water upwards. Any point betwixt *H* and *D*, being in descent; but yet the more the Screw declines downwards towards *D*, by so much the more water will be carried up by it.

If you would know the just quantity of water which every revolution does contain and carry, according to any inclination of the Cylinder, this may be easily found by ascribing on it an *Ellipsis*, parallel to the Horizon; which *Ellipsis* will shew how much of the revolution is empty, and how much full.

See a further explication of this in *Ubaldus de Cochlea, l. 2. prop. 25.*

The

Cap. 15. *Mechanical Motions.*

The true inclination of the Screw being found, together with the certain quantity of water which every *Helix* does contain; it is further considerable, that the water by this Instrument does ascend naturally of it self without any violence or labour, and that the heaviness of it doth lie chiefly upon the centers or axis of the Cylinder, both its sides being of equal weight (saith *Ubaldus*); So that (it should seem) though we suppose each revolution to have an equal quantity of water, yet the Screw will remain with any part upwards (according as it shall be set) without turning it self either way. And therefore the least strength being added to either of its sides, should make it descend, according to that common Maxime of *Archimedes*; any addition will make that which equiponderates with another, to tend downwards.

Ibid. l. 3. prop. 4.

De Equipond. Suppos. 2.

But now, because the weight of this instrument, and the water in it, does lean wholly upon the axis, hence

hence is it (faith *Ubaldus*) that the grating and rubbing of these axes against the sockets wherein they are placed, will cause some ineptitude and resistency to that rotation of the Cylinder, which would otherwise ensue upon the addition of the least weight to any one side; But (faith the same Author) any power that is greater than this resistency which does arise from the axis, will serve for the turning of it round.

These things considered together, it will hence appear, how a perpetual motion may seem easily contrivable. For if there were but such a water-wheel made on this instrument, upon which the stream that is carried up, may fall, in its descent it would turn the screw round, and by that means convey as much water up, as is required to move it; so that the motion must needs be continual, since the same weight which in its fall does turn the wheel, is by the turning of the wheel carried up again.

Or if the water falling upon one wheel,

wheel, would not be forcible enough for this effect, why then there might be two or three, or more, according as the length and elevation of the inſtrument will admit; By which means the weight of it may be ſo multiplied in the fall, that it ſhall be equivalent to twice or thrice that quantity of water which aſcends. As may be more plainly diſcerned by this following Diagram.

Where

Dædalus; or, Lib. II.

Cap. 15. *Mechanical Motions.*

Where the figure *L M*, at the bottome does represent a wooden Cylinder with Helical cavities cut in it, which at *A B*, is supposed to be covered over with tin plates, and three water-wheels upon it, *H I K*. The lower cistern which contains the water being *C D*. Now this Cylinder being turned round, all the water which from the cistern ascends thro' it, will fall into the vessel at *E*, and from that vessel being conveyed upon the water-wheel *H*, shall consequently give a circular motion to the whole Screw: Or if this alone should be too weak for the turning of it, then the same water which falls from the wheel *H*, being received into the other vessel *F*, may from thence again descend on the wheel *I*; by which means the force of it will be doubled. And if this be yet insufficient, then may the water which falls on the second wheel *I*, be received into the other vessel *G*, and from thence again descend on the third wheel at *K*: and so for as many

There is another like contrivance to this purpose in *Pet. Bettin. Apiar.* 4. *Progym.* 1. *Prop.* 10. but with much less advantage than 'tis here proposed.

many other wheels, as the instrument is capable of. So that besides the greater distance of these three streams from the center or axis, by which they are made so much heavier; and besides, that the fall of this outward water is forcible and violent, whereas the ascent of that within, is natural; Besides all this, there is thrice as much water to turn the Screw, as is carried up by it.

But on the other side, if all the water falling upon one wheel, would be able to turn it round, then half of it would serve with two wheels; and the rest may be so disposed of in the fall, as to serve unto some other useful delightful ends.

When I first thought of this invention, I could scarce forbear with *Archimedes* to cry out εὕρηκα εὕρηκα; It seeming so infallible a way for the effecting of a perpetual motion, that nothing could be so much as probably objected against it: But upon trial and experience I find it altogether insufficient for any such purpose

Cap. 15. *Mechanical Motions.*

purpose, and that for these two reasons:

1. The water that ascends, will not make any considerable stream in the fall.

2. This stream (though multiplied) will not be of force enough to turn about the Screw.

1. The water ascends gently, and by intermissions, but it falls continuately, and with force; each of the three vessels being supposed full at the first, that so the weight of the water in them might add the greater strength and swiftness to the streams that descend from them. Now this swiftness of motion will cause so great a difference betwixt them, that one of these little streams may spend more water in the fall, than a stream six times bigger in the ascent, though we should suppose both of them to be continuate; How much more then, when as the ascending water is vented by fits and intermissions, every circumvolution voiding only so much as is contained

tained in one *Helix*? And in this particular, one that is not versed in these kind of experiments, may be easily deceived.

But secondly, though there were so great a disproportion, yet notwithstanding the force of these outward streams might well enough serve for the turning of the Screw, if it were so that both its sides would equiponderate, the water being in them (as *Ubaldus* hath affirmed). But now upon farther examination, we shall find this assertion of his, to be utterly against both reason and experience. And herein does consist the chief mistake of this contrivance. For the ascending side of the Screw is made by the water contained in it, so much heavier than the descending side, that these outward streams thus applied, will not be of force enough to make them equiponderate, much less to move the whole. As may be more easily discerned by this figure.

Where

Cap. 15. *Mechanical Motions.*

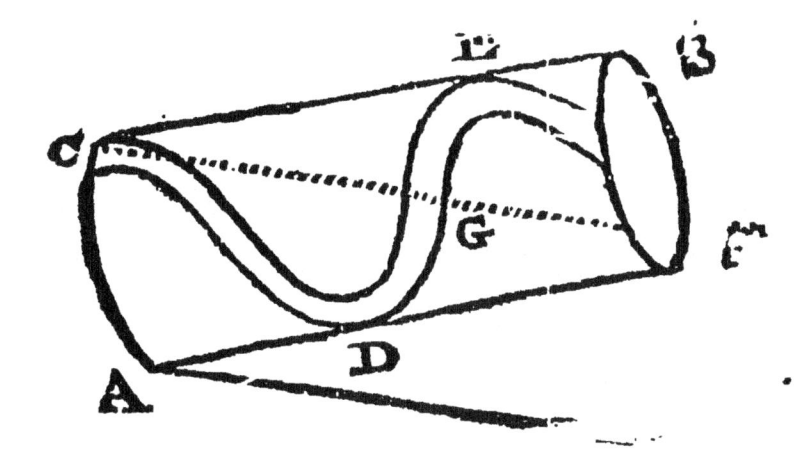

Where *A B*, represents a Screw covered over, *C D E* one *Helix* or revolution of it, *C D* the ascending side, *E D* the descending side, the point *D* the middle. The Horizontal line *C F*, shewing how much of the *Helix* is filled with water, *viz.* of the ascending side, from *C* the beginning of the *Helix*, to *D* the middle of it; and on the descending side, from *D* the middle, to the point *G*, where the Horizontal does cut the *Helix*. Now it is evident, that this latter part *D G*, is nothing near so much, and consequently not so heavy as the other *D C*. And thus is it in all the other revolutions, which as they are either more, or larger, so

will

will the difficulty of this motion be increased. Whence it will appear, that the outward streams which descend, must be of so much force as to countervail all that weight whereby the ascending side in every one of these revolutions does exceed the other; And though this may be effected by making the water-wheels larger; yet then the motion will be so slow, that the Screw will not be able to supply the outward streams.

There is another contrivance to this purpose mentioned by *Kircher de Magnete*, *l.* 2. *p.* 4. depending upon the heat of the Sun, and the force of winds; but it is liable to such abundance of exceptions, that it is scarce worth the mentioning, and does by no means deserve the confidence of any ingenious Artist.

Thus have I briefly explained the probabilities and defects of those subtil contrivances, whereby the making of a perpetual motion hath been attempted. I would be loth to discourage the enquiry of any ingenious Artificer,

Cap. 15. *Mechanical Motions.*

Artificer, by denying the possibility of effecting it with any of these Mechanical helps; but yet (I conceive) if those principles which concern the slowness of the power in comparison to the greatness of the weight, were rightly understood, and throughly considered, they would make this experiment to seem (if not altogether impossible, yet) much more difficult than otherwise perhaps it will appear. However, the inquiring after it, cannot but deserve our endeavours, as being one of the most noble amongst all these Mechanical subtilties. And (as it is in the fable of him who dug the Vineyard for a hid treasure, though he did not find the money, yet he thereby made the ground more fruitful; so) though we do not attain to the effecting of this particular, yet our searching after it may discover so many other excellent subtilties, as shall abundantly recompence the labour of our enquiry.

And then besides, it may be another encouragement to consider the
pleasure

Treated of before, l. 1

Dædalus; or, Lib. II.

pleasure of such speculations, which do ravish and sublime the thoughts with more clear Angelical contentments. *Archimedes* was generally so taken up in the delight of these Mathematical studies of this familiar *Siren*, (as *Plutarch* stiles them) that he forgot both his meat and drink, and other necessities of nature; nay, that he neglected the saving of his life, when that rude soldier in the pride and haste of victory, would not give him leasure to finish his demonstration. What a ravishment was that, when having found out the way to measure *Hiero's* Crown, he leaped out of the Bath, and (as if he were suddenly possest) ran naked up and down, crying εὕρηκα. εὕρηκα.! It is storied of *Thales*, that in his joy and gratitude for one of these Mathematical inventions, he went presently to the Temple, and there offered up a solemn sacrifice. And *Pythagoras* upon the like occasion is related to have sacrificed a hundred Oxen. The justice of providence having

οἰκείας ϗ συνοίκου σειρῆνος.
Plutarch Marcell.
Joan. Tzetzes, Chil. Hist. 35.
Valer. Maxim. l. 8. c. 7.

Cap. 15. *Mechanical Motions.*

ving so contrived it, that the pleasure which there is in the success of such inventions, should be proportioned to the great difficulty and labour of their inquiry.

FINIS.

CPSIA information can be obtained
at www.ICGtesting.com
Printed in the USA
LVOW03s1533060516
487047LV00001B/4/P